HOW TO SURVIVE WITHOUT A JOB

Practical solutions for developing skills and building self-esteem

Ursula Markham

PIATKUS

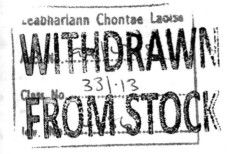

Contents

To Philip and David,
with my love

What the caterpillar calls the end of the world,
the master calls a butterfly.

RICHARD BACH, *Illusions*

Introduction

There may be many reasons why you find yourself with too much time and too little to do.

Perhaps – in common with so many others – you have been made redundant; or you might have left school or college only to find yourself unable to get a job in the first place. You may have retired – either because you chose to do so or because you were compelled to upon reaching a certain age.

You may have spent years bringing up a family, or caring for an elderly or sick person, only to find time stretching before you now that your ministrations are no longer needed; or perhaps ill-health or disability confines you to your home and its immediate surroundings.

Whatever the reason, you are likely to be experiencing a range of confusing emotions, some of which may surprise or distress you. And these emotions in turn can affect your physical well-being, so that you do not feel fit enough to face the future positively . . .

Stop! Let's see what we can do to turn things around. Of course I cannot offer you a job in the accepted sense of paid employment. What I *can* do, however, is help you to come to terms with all those feelings, to see yourself and your role in life in a new light, and to look forward to the future with hope, joy and optimism.

It is easier than you might think. And even if your life does not turn out as you once expected it to, it can still be busy, fulfilled and well worth living.

— 1 —

It's OK to have feelings

Sometimes we have no control over the 'slings and arrows' life hurls at us. Like it or not, there are certain situations we are compelled to accept. Being in the position of having no specific job to do – paid or otherwise – may be one of these situations. At such times the hardest thing is often to acknowledge our own feelings.

There may be many reasons for this enforced situation. At the present time there are literally millions of people who would dearly love to be in paid employment, but who, through no fault of their own, cannot find a job. Not only are there those who have been made redundant – often at an age when, despite their years of experience, short-sighted employers consider them 'too old' to be offered work – but there are also vast numbers of young people leaving schools, colleges and universities who are unable to find work of any sort (let alone the type of work they were hoping for).

As life expectancy increases, so does the number of healthy years a person may hope to live after retirement. For those people who have been longing for more time to devote to long-established hobbies and interests, this may be a great blessing; but for many who find themselves less well prepared those same years may appear as an endless, barren desert stretching before them. In many cases, of course, retirement was not even voluntary but was summarily forced upon the individual by company policy.

For the woman whose time has long been filled with looking after a growing family – whether or not she also had a job – the time when the last child finally leaves home can come as quite a shock. She may have been telling herself for years that she is looking forward to this day so that she can spend more time on herself and her own interests. Why, then, does she feel this sudden sense of loss and lack of purpose?

There are some people whose disability or physical frailty makes it difficult – or even impossible – for them to leave their homes or take up employment on a regular basis. They, too, may look at the years ahead of them with fear or anxiety.

Whatever the situation, there are certain emotions which are common to all those I have mentioned. Unease, dread, a sense of being 'useless' – all these may be experienced by each of those people. There will also be a whole range of feelings peculiar to each category. Whatever the cause of your current situation, acknowledging those feelings and coming to terms with them is an essential first step on the road to a positive outlook.

It is very important to take stock of the kaleidoscope of your current emotions. Some people, particularly after redundancy, find it easier to push everything to the back of their mind and try to continue as if they had no feelings at all. This works in the very short term, but failure to acknowledge and consider your deepest feelings can often lead to long-term problems. You become like a pressure cooker from which the steam has no escape outlet – eventually something has to give. And often that 'something' is your physical or mental health.

So the first thing you should do is make time to think about the way you feel. Don't worry whether or not you think you are right to feel this way – just be absolutely honest about your emotions. If you can find someone to talk them over with, so much the better. But, even if there is no one, it is essential to deal with your feelings if you are to go on with life in a positive way.

Feeling that you have nothing specific to do can come upon you suddenly, can send out warning signals which you may or may not act upon, or it can creep up on you almost unnoticed. Here are some of the causes of this situation.

Redundancy

There is no easy way of making someone redundant but, while some employers do all they can to soften the blow, others appear to be completely heartless in outlook. Here are just three examples from many I have come across in the past year or two:

MARK

Mark was a sales representative for a large manufacturing organisation. Although he knew that sales were down a little on the previous year, he had no idea that the company itself was getting into deep financial difficulty.

One Tuesday afternoon in spring Mark was driving along a coast road in Dorset travelling from one appointment to another. He pulled into a lay-by so that he could telephone an order through to head office. Having done so, he was just about to switch off his mobile phone when the voice at the other end of the line said 'Oh, and by the way, you're redundant from Friday'.

That was it. No letter, no kind words, no thanks for his services, no commiseration. Just a single, cold sentence from a distant, disembodied voice.

Mark told me afterwards that he did not know how he managed to complete his calls that day. All he was aware of was a tight feeling in his chest, and an ever-rising sense of panic as he thought about his mortgage and his family.

ANNIE

Annie worked for the British section of an American-owned direct marketing organisation in the north of England. One day, along with the other nine members of her department, she was called to a 4 pm meeting in the chairman's office. They were given no clue as to the purpose of this meeting and, no one from the management team being present, they simply stood around looking at one another, waiting for something to happen.

After about ten minutes a young clerical assistant came into the room clutching a bundle of envelopes. Silently she handed one to each member of the assembled group. Filled with a sudden sense of foreboding, Annie could feel her heart racing as she tore open her envelope with shaking hands. Inside were three pieces of paper: a cheque for a month's salary, a letter of reference, and a note telling her that she was redundant from that moment on and that she could not even return to clear her desk – someone else was in the process of doing this for her.

One look at the stricken faces around her was enough to tell Annie that her colleagues' envelopes had contained similar information. Distressed as she was, she found herself looking round at those members of the department who had families to support. She was devastated by the unexpected blow, but at least she was young and single with no real responsibilities. She might have to give up her rented flat and move back with her parents until she found another job but what, she wondered, would happen to people like Eric – 49 years old, married with four teenage children. What chance did he stand of getting another job?

PAUL

Paul was 22 and worked with two others of similar age in the computer design department of an engineering company. They all knew that the company had been experiencing difficulties and had spoken among themselves about the possibility of redundancies being necessary some time in the future. But none of them was prepared for the blow when it struck.

The personnel officer came in to speak to them at the beginning of one week. She told them that the firm was not in danger of closing, but that it had become necessary to make some cutbacks, one of which would be in their department. In future only two people were to be employed there rather than the three they had now. Since the board could not decide which one should have to go, it had been left to them to come to their own decision. Would they please tell her by the end of the week which one of them was accepting redundancy?

The young men could not believe what they heard. How could they make such a decision? Which one of them was going to say that he was willing to put himself out of work? It was an impossible situation and should never have been forced upon them. Eventually Friday came and, the young men having been unable to make the decision, one of them was summarily fired. It was Paul.

Being made redundant is a devastating experience for anyone – even when they have been half expecting it. You may know that lay-offs are more commonly related to the state of the company balance sheet than to the talent and ability of any individual. You may realise that you are in the same boat as armies of other people. You may have heard that some of the greatest names in business have come through redundancy, and gone on to bigger and better things. None of those pieces of knowledge can deflect the initial blow you experience when you realise that, in the eyes of your employers, you are definitely dispensable.

After the immediate sense of shock, people tend to react in one of several ways. One person will feel a sense of shame as though being made redundant is some sort of disgrace which will lower them in the eyes of others. Another will become very, very angry and aggressive. One will immediately go into a frenzy of action – sending off applications and CVs in every direction. The other will stay indoors and brood, even having difficulty in finding a reason for getting out of bed in the morning.

However you deal with the blow when it falls, you are likely to find that, once this initial reaction has passed, you have a tendency to experience dramatic mood swings. You may fluctuate daily between a sense of high optimism and one of deep despair. Be assured that you are not alone – this is quite a normal reaction to a difficult situation.

It is very important to take time to think about how you feel and to talk about those feelings to those closest to you. If your redundancy is a source of anxiety to you, it will also cause anxiety in your partner – whether or not he or she has a job. No one likes to see the person they care for suffering, but it is very difficult to be loving and supportive to someone who appears to be shutting you out. So, once the immediate shock has passed, find a quiet time together and be as honest as you can about your feelings. If your confidence and self-esteem have been reduced, say so. If you don't know how you are going to manage financially, say so. If you are afraid that you will appear less worthy of love and respect, say so. There is a great sense of relief in honesty with those who are special to you and, even though it may not solve your current problems, it may go a long way towards preventing them leading to complications in your relationship.

If you have no one close to you with whom you feel you can discuss your innermost feelings, perhaps you could seek the assistance of a professional counsellor – preferably one who specialises in redundancy counselling. It is a sad sign of our times that there are a growing number of counselling organisations who are able to provide such a service.

Even if you choose not to speak to anyone else about how you feel, do be honest with yourself. Write down your emotions and your reasons for them. Somehow, once something is down on paper, it becomes a task to be accomplished rather than an insurmountable lifelong problem.

You have been through a crisis situation and there are certain steps to be taken in dealing with any crisis. Following these may help you to come to terms with what has happened.

1 *Evaluate the situation* What are the immediate consequences of what has happened? Assess your own feelings about the situation.

2 *What are your objectives?*   To find another job? To set up in business for yourself? What do you want to achieve?

3 *What are the immediate priorities?*   Perhaps you will want to seek advice, bearing your objectives in mind. Even if you have received a generous financial settlement, you do not know how long the current situation will last, so you might need to make some changes in the family budget. If you have a mortgage or a loan, it is important to let the lenders know what has happened so that any necessary adjustments can be made.

4 *Make plans*   You could make enquiries about retraining if you felt this was appropriate. Or you could look on the redundancy as an opportunity to do something you have always yearned to do.

5 *Put those plans into action – starting now!*   The sooner you make a start – even if all you do at this stage is seek further information – the sooner you will feel that you are back in control of your own future.

6 *Communicate*   In addition to talking about your feelings, it is a good idea to let other people know about your situation. Many a new opportunity has arisen through this sort of networking.

By taking positive steps such as these, your self-esteem will begin to rise and this will stand you in good stead when it comes to possible future interviews.

—— *Lack of job opportunities* —— *for the young*

So there you are, just out of school, college or university, ready to take your place in the world of the employed . . . only that world doesn't seem to want you. All the years of acquiring education, skills and knowledge seem to have been purposeless if you cannot find a job at the end of them. You look around and see others who have been in this position for a year or two – and you wonder what to do.

Unfortunately this is a situation which is becoming more and more common. Further education is no longer necessarily the answer; many 18- or 21-year-old school or college leavers are finding it just as difficult to obtain employment as those who finish their education at 16.

This was the position in which Andrew found himself when I spoke to him. He had completed his course at the local college some nine months earlier and had been trying ever since to find a job – but with no success. He was beginning to feel that the situation was hopeless.

He told me that one of the hardest things to cope with was the attitude of other people. Andrew believed that everyone else considered him to be an idle layabout with no desire to work, happy to live on 'handouts' from the State. Now, I do not know whether other people had *really* formed this opinion of Andrew or whether he simply believed this to be the case because he himself felt so desperate. But whichever it was did not matter; the fact that Andy believed it to be so was sufficient to create the air of negativity which hung around him like a cloud.

Young people like Andrew, who may have grown up in a world where they were encouraged to want to do and acquire things which cost money, suddenly find that they have barely enough to live on and certainly too little to spend much on enjoyment. Records, CDs, discos, holidays, cars . . . all these cost more money than they are likely to have at their disposal. Of course they know that they can live without these things, but it is not easy when they see others more fortunate than themselves who have jobs, and can afford some of the treats and luxuries of life.

Even more difficult to cope with is the prospect of the months of unemployment turning into years. Suppose you never get a job – after all, how do you compile a CV detailing your past experience when no one has given you the chance to acquire any? And if you don't find employment and never have any money, how are you to find a partner, make a home and raise a family?

Andrew loved the countryside and was a keen walker. As walking is an inexpensive hobby, he often used to set out for the day, sometimes alone and sometimes with friends. Imagine how hurtful he found it when an unthinking neighbour criticised him for 'being off enjoying himself instead of out looking for work'.

As with people who have been made redundant, it is necessary for those in Andrew's position to pause and assess how they feel. It is also vital to realise that all their feelings are understandable and not an indication that there is something wrong with them.

Later on in this book you will find information on things you can do which cost very little and which may, in addition, go some way towards providing the 'experience' so often requested in job application forms. For now, let's have a look at some of the more common emotions of those who find themselves in the same situation as Andrew.

ANGER

Unemployed young people may feel cheated after spending years at school and possibly in further education. Many will have been encouraged by parents or teachers to head in a certain direction because they were 'sure to get a good job', so they feel let down by individuals and angry at the world. This is perfectly understandable. If it affects you, make a list of all the aspects of your current situation which arouse anger in you and ask yourself whether the anger is justified. At the time the advice was given, it may well have been impossible to foresee the way things would turn out; is it fair to be angry at people who were genuinely giving you the best advice they could – even if that advice turned out to be ill-founded?

It is important, too, to realise that anger is an energy and an extremely forceful one. What a waste of your own inner strength and power to allow it to turn into anger when it could just as well be used to create a positive energy which could be beneficial to you in many ways.

SHAME

No matter how many times you tell Andrew or his companions that they have nothing to be ashamed of and that they are not responsible for the current lack of employment opportunities, none the less, as you have seen, they do feel that others are looking down on them and thinking of them as idlers who have no intention of trying to get a job. If this is how you feel, ask yourself whether you have been shown signs that this is how others regard you or whether it is possible that, because your self-esteem has taken a beating, you simply *believe* this to be the case. If you know that you are right, consider whether you have been doing all you can to improve the situation. Knowing that you have will enable you to take pride in yourself and should help you not to allow the mistaken views of others to affect you.

FEAR

Of course you are frightened. You are frightened that you might never have a job, that no one will ever want to love or care for you, that you will never be able to acquire all those ordinary things which contribute to everyday life. But, just as anger is a negative use of strong energy, it is important to realise that fear can bind and shackle you in such a way that you are quite unable to think clearly or to make those decisions which might help you escape from your current situation.

Make a list of your fears and then prioritise them. Now see what you can do to tackle any of the items on your list. Is your greatest fear that you are destined to be alone because you cannot afford to go to the type of place where people meet? You need to realise that there are many others in the same situation and that there are endless opportunities for meeting other people which can be fun and which don't need to cost money. Are you frightened that you will never be able to get a job? If so, what are the positive things you can do? You might decide to change direction and train in an area where there are more prospects. Facing your fears and trying to do something to allay them brings an improvement in your self-image and a sense of positivity.

BOREDOM

Does the endlessly long week seem to consist of seven endlessly long days? What are you going to do about it – assuming that you do not like this feeling? Think about your interests: you may have to adapt them to fit in with your present financial situation, but you do not have to abandon them altogether. Music can be borrowed from libraries. Friends can dance together to the sound of a cassette player. Talking costs nothing at all.

—— *Parents whose children* —— *have left home*

Although it is usually hardest on the mother, both parents can experience a sense of loss when the last of their children leaves home and there are fathers who are single parents, as well as those who stay at home and care for the family while their wife goes out to work. What follows, therefore, can apply to both men and women, although in the majority of instances it is likely to be the latter.

Even in the career-minded 1990s, there are still many mothers who spend much of their time caring for the home and family. They may have jobs, whether part-time or full-time, or they may have chosen to devote several years of their lives to bringing up their children. Whichever is the case, their days will have been well occupied – particularly if there are several children in the family.

Eventually the time comes when the last of those children leaves home to go to college, to undergo some form of training, to travel abroad or simply to set up home on their own. On the one hand the mother may be delighted to see her youngest son or daughter go off into the world but, on the other, there is the inevitable sense of loss. Days which used to be so full suddenly seem to have great gulfs of emptiness which she is unsure of filling.

This is usually a period of confused emotions for the woman concerned. She may feel that she has accomplished what was meant to be her major task and this can cause her to feel that the rest of her life has comparatively little purpose. The last people she can express these feelings to may be the children themselves; if she has any sensitivity at all, the thing she would not want is to run the risk of making them feel that she was not happy for them or to cause them to feel guilty for leaving home. Because she is told by certain areas of the media that all women should find fulfilment outside the home, she may not like to admit that she has really enjoyed being a mother and caring for her family. As she reads certain newspapers and magazines, it is easy to imagine that every other woman has reached the stage where her independence and her career mean more to her than anything else. And, of course, for some women this is true – and it is appropriate that it should be. But it is just as appropriate for others to find their fulfilment in caring for the family.

Helen was just such a woman. She had worked in a local department store almost all her married life, but her real joy had been in her family – her husband Brian and her three children. She had been quite content with her job; the other members of staff were friendly and the money was certainly useful, but she was not particularly ambitious and was happy to leave all thoughts of work behind at the end of the day.

Finally the day arrived when her younger son set off to join the merchant navy and, although she had obviously known that the day was coming, Helen was quite unprepared for the emotions which overtook her. She felt lost and unwanted – although logic told her she still had the love of Brian and the children – and a little frightened of the future. She also felt annoyed with herself for entertaining these feelings and ashamed that she was not like all these bright, career-oriented women she kept hearing about.

It was important for Helen to realise that all her feelings were natural and did not make her in any way inferior to other people. She did not know what she wanted to do with the rest of her life and did not feel up to making such a decision.

If you find yourself feeling as Helen did, there is no harm in taking a little time to pause and take stock, and even to pamper yourself a little. It is all part of putting yourself high on your list of priorities again – something you may not have done for quite some time. Then, when you are feeling more relaxed, you can begin to consider the future and how you feel about it.

Perhaps, now that you have more time, you would like to return to work or change your job. One of the things which frightens many women who have been at home for a few years is the amount of technological change which has taken place in the working world since they left it. You may have left an office as a shorthand-typist only to find that world is now a high-tech one of computers, fax machines and IT (information technology). Even the once-simple cash register has disappeared in favour of an all-singing, all-dancing state-of-the-art monster. If you have never handled a computer or word processor, of course you are going to feel uneasy, but there are many different types of courses specially designed for women who want to return to work. Taking such a course before even applying for jobs would help to boost your self-confidence, which in turn will stand you in good stead when it comes to applications and interviews. There are too many women whose lack of confidence causes them to sell themselves short and settle for a lesser position than their abilities equip them for.

Of course, you may not wish to change your job or return to work, but you may still be wondering how to fill all those extra hours you suddenly seem to have. Pause a moment to realise that you are at a very exciting stage of your life when many possibilities lie before you. Perhaps you will decide to do some form of voluntary work, spend some time studying or indulge in one or more hobbies. What you do is up to you. It is a matter of assessing what you like doing, what you are good at and seeing to what conclusions those considerations lead you.

Retirement

Some people choose to take early retirement, while others are prised, kicking and screaming, from their jobs at an age decided by company policy. Whichever is the case, it could lead to resentment and a sense of uselessness. Even those who have been looking forward to the day they could retire may find themselves with more time on their hands than they had bargained for.

Naturally there are those people who revel in their retirement – who cannot think how they ever found the time to go to work in the first place. Their days are full of interest and opportunity, and they look forward to enjoying a long and happy future. They may be able to pursue hobbies and interests or spend more time with members of their family.

Others, however, feel even more cut off from their families as they grow older. This is an essentially Western phenomenon, since in the East people tend to be treated with more and more respect as they grow older. Richard Blackwell, president of the Register of Chinese Herbal Medicine, recently said on this subject:

There is also a respect for old people, unlike other races. As Chinese people get older, they take on a more important role in the family. That clearly is good for the health and general feeling of well-being. The opposite can be seen in those people who die fairly soon after retirement when there is a feeling of being thrown on the scrapheap.

Even someone who has chosen to retire may find themselves with too much time and too little to do. They may experience feelings of regret that the 'best' part of their life has gone. They may grow angry, knowing that they are still capable of doing far more than opportunity allows. If this negativity is allowed to grow and fester, they will become more ill humoured, taking their feelings out on those around them. This, in turn, will make them unpopular so that people will tend to avoid them – which only causes the negative feelings to increase.

If, on the other hand, you have been compelled to retire earlier than you would have wished, you may experience all the emotions already mentioned plus a sense of resentment that you have been cast aside against your will. If, to add to that, you have been a workaholic in the past, you may even experience symptoms of depression or problems with your health.

We are tending to live to a greater age now than people did a generation or two ago, so retirement is often longer and this may cause you to experience fears about the future. Some of these fears will be financial while others will be emotional. You may be concerned about being considered 'over the hill', worry about an increasing lack of independence or possible problems with your health. Naturally you should do all you can to ensure your financial and physical well-being where possible but, having done that, it is important to acknowledge and accept the worries – then put them aside and get on with living. Brian Livesley, professor in the care of the elderly at London University, says:

Taking a positive mental attitude to retirement is important. Among 65 year olds, less than 4% are in hospital or institutions. This figure only rises at 85, so why worry when you retire at 60 or 65? Most people survive to at least 75 and at 60 or 65 you face twenty years of good health.

2

Steps to stress reduction

Whatever your situation, it is important, once you have acknow-ledged your feelings, to do something about becoming more positive – which is what this book should help you to do. If you don't, you might find yourself suffering physically as well as emotionally. For one thing is certain – your state of mind can definitely affect your state of health.

Orthodox Western medicine is now coming to accept what Eastern philosophies and practitioners of complementary medi-cine have known for years – that our emotions play a great part in the condition of our physical health. In some cases negative emotions can actually be responsible for the break-down of the physical condition (as in irritable bowel syndrome which, it is now accepted, can, in some cases, be the direct result of anxiety and distress): in others they greatly exacerbate an existing condi-tion (attacks of eczema, psoriasis, migraine and asthma often break out after a period of extreme stress).

Dr Candace Pert of Rutgers University in the US has done a great deal of research on the effect of the emotions on the physical health of the patient. She has found that chemical messengers called neuropeptides are affected by our feelings and that these neuropeptides can cause chemical changes which alter the state of the body's immune system, either weakening or strengthening it.

We all know how harmful excess stress can be to the mind and body of the individual – but we tend to link stress with those people who are so busy that they are under extreme pressure. We do not always think of it in connection with those who appear to have too much time and too few ways of filling it. And yet, feelings of loneliness, anger, frustration, bitterness and resentment . . . these are some of the greatest causes of excess stress.

By using this book, I hope you are going to discover ways of making your life more positive and fulfilling – and therefore less stressful. But, in the mean time, it is important to try and counteract the stress already caused by the negative emotions you have understandably been experiencing. And, even if you are not yet able to let those emotions go, at least you can be taking the following steps to prevent them having a harmful effect on your physical well-being.

Nutrition

This is one area of your life where you can be in control. You will be better able to withstand the physical effects of stress if you are taking in the appropriate proteins, vitamins and minerals. There are plenty of books available to give you information about which foods contain which vitamins and what is the correct daily quantity needed. If you find that you really dislike a particular range of foods so that you are not able to absorb enough of the vitamin or mineral contained in them, you could always take it in supplement form.

There is no need to stick to an impossibly strict regime; the occasional lapse into junk food is going to do you no long-term harm. But, if you are aware that you are going through a particularly stressful period in your life, that is the time to take extra care. Nor is it necessary to spend a great deal of money to eat healthily. In fact, some of the most nutritious items are also some of the cheapest – rice, pulses, beans, fruits and vegetables in season etc. And the cheaper types of fish and cuts of meat can be just as nutritious as steak and salmon.

Sleep

One of the commonest signs of troubled emotions is often the inability to sleep. Or perhaps you sleep fitfully, only to wake feeling unrefreshed and irritable.

Sound sleep can be extremely therapeutic; it is the natural healer of the mind and body. The length of time is unimportant – we don't all need eight hours' sleep a night. What does matter is that you sleep soundly, and wake feeling fit and able to face the day.

There is no point lying there willing yourself to 'go to sleep' – this just does not work. In fact the tension caused by your failure and frustration will simply tend to increase the stress-related problem. If you are finding it difficult to sleep because of your emotional turmoil, here are a few hints which might make it easier.

- Don't go to bed when you feel wide awake. Stay up and read (not horror books) or listen to music until you begin to feel drowsy.

- Be sure to take some sort of physical exercise during the day; brisk walking is sufficient.

- Avoid caffeinated drinks too late at night as these will keep you awake.

- You may be tempted to have a drink to help you sleep but you will find that, although alcohol may indeed help you to fall asleep in the first place, you are likely to wake up again after an hour or two.

- Have a warm (not hot!) bath before retiring.

- Don't smoke (or allow anyone else to do so) in the bedroom. Quite apart from the harmful effects of smoking, it will make the room stuffy and you will find it harder to sleep.

- Make yourself a warm drink – perhaps hot chocolate, milk or a herbal tea such as camomile which encourages sleep.

- Establish a pre-bedtime routine. If you always do the same things in the same order before retiring, your subconscious mind will become attuned to the fact that you will soon be going to sleep.

- Once in bed, practise a relaxation technique. You will find one detailed below, but there are many others which can be learned from books or cassettes.

Exercise

When you exercise your circulation improves and you reduce the amount of lactic acid in your body. Since lactic acid induces mental and physical exhaustion (as opposed to a pleasant tiredness), it tends to increase the amount of stress you feel.

The form of exercise you choose depends entirely upon your preference. You don't have to go jogging if this is something you hate. In fact it doesn't have to be the same form of exercise every time. But, whatever it is, it is really important to find something you enjoy or you will never stick to it. And, if you can exercise with family or friends, or in a group, you can make it much more fun.

The best form of exercise is regular and controlled. And you should start slowly – particularly if you are not used to physical exercise. Perhaps try a basic stretching routine or a walk around the block to begin with. And, if you have any doubts at all about your fitness for exercising, do consult your physician before you begin.

Exercise is also good for your heart as your overall blood pressure is reduced and your coronary blood vessels expand, preventing them from becoming blocked.

Isometric exercises (such as weight training) are not as beneficial as aerobic exercises (such as cycling). Isometric exercises are excellent for improving muscle tone, but they don't encourage you to breathe more deeply and they can actually increase tension, whereas aerobic exercises help to increase your oxygen intake.

Breathing

Naturally, you have been breathing all your life – but how many of us actually take the time to breathe *properly?* How are you breathing right now? Probably, in common with most people, your breathing is coming mainly from the upper chest area rather than from your diaphragm.

Breathing in supplies oxygen while breathing out eliminates carbon dioxide and wastes from the system. If this carbon dioxide is not removed, your cells will eventually become contaminated.

It is a fact that most people use only 50 per cent of their breathing potential. This means they are absorbing only 50 per cent of their oxygen potential and (what is worse) only eliminating 50 per cent of their carbon dioxide. Anyone who has taken part in regular exercise will tell you that, even when physically tired, they feel really good afterwards. Exercise, of course, compels you to breathe deeply and well, and this accounts for the sense of well-being which ensues.

Therapists have achieved great success with some forms of depression by teaching their patients to breathe properly. Perhaps our grandparents had the right idea when they encouraged us to fling open the window and take several deep breaths at the start of the day. (Although if you live in an area of high pollution, this might not be such a good thing to do!)

It is perhaps easier to see the link between breathing and the emotions. When someone is experiencing panic, their breathing becomes shallow and rapid; extreme cases can induce hyperventilation. This also works in reverse as experiments have shown that if an individual deliberately hyperventilates he or she will actually become panicky over nothing and could even pass out.

So, if you are aware of tension within you when faced with a particular worry, stop and make yourself breathe slowly and regularly, and you will find yourself more able to think clearly and therefore more likely to gain control over the situation.

Relaxation

There are many different relaxation techniques, but the one which follows is simple, effective and need only take ten minutes of your time. You can, of course, practise it as often as you feel is necessary but, if it is to be helpful in reducing your stress level, you should do it at least once every day.

First, make sure that you are comfortable. You could lie on your bed or on the floor, or you can sit in a chair – but, if so, do make sure that it has a high enough back to support your head and neck. The temperature should be warm but not too hot and you should be on your own if possible so that you can work at your own speed. Then progress through the following stages.

1 Close your eyes and, starting with your feet and working upwards, tense and relax each set of muscles in turn. Pay particular attention to those around your neck and jaw as this is where the most stress tends to be experienced.

2 Spend a few moments breathing deeply and evenly. Make sure you feel your rib-cage expanding so that you are not simply breathing from the upper chest.

3 Now create a picture in your mind of a place you find beautiful – it can be a real spot or an imaginary one. See it in as much detail as possible, trying to involve all your senses. What does it look like? What sounds would you expect to hear? etc. Don't stand still. In your imagination wander around that place so that you come to know it from every angle.

4 Stay in your chosen place for several minutes before quietly opening your eyes. Sit or lie still for a few moments before getting up. (Or, if you are having difficulty sleeping, you could practise this technique in bed and just allow yourself to drift off to sleep afterwards.)

So, whatever the reason for the emotions you are feeling, take the time to acknowledge them and, if appropriate, to accept that experiencing them is quite understandable. Bring them out in the open by talking about them if possible (or perhaps writing them down). Having examined them, only you can decide whether you intend to concentrate on them to the potential detriment of your health or whether you intend to set about making some changes in your outlook on life by becoming more positive. And be sure of this – you do have the ability to make those changes, and to live a happier and fuller life.

3

I'm a terrific person!

One of the things which happens to everyone who would really rather have a job but is without one is that their self-esteem plunges. This is unfortunate enough if you are someone who normally has quite a positive self-image but, if you happen to be one of those people whose opinion of themselves happens to be more negative, you could really find yourself wallowing in a morass of despondency.

Personal self-esteem can be such a fragile thing and yet it colours every aspect of your life. The way you feel about yourself can affect your family, your work, your relationships and your health. And, of course, when any or all of those suffer, you feel even worse about yourself – and so you find that you are caught up in a vicious circle of negativity.

Psychologists in the US claim that two out of every three people suffer from low self-esteem. This is really sad when you realise that it is one aspect of yourself about which it is possible to do something positive. You may not be able to control all the events which surround your life, but you can have control over your outlook and the way in which you allow those events to affect you. No matter what the circumstances, it is possible to feel motivated and excited by life again.

In this chapter we are going to do a mini-course in improving self-esteem. No, it won't find you a job; nor will it provide the answer to any on-going problems around you. What it will do is make you able to deal positively with the present and empower you to look forward to the future.

Think about yourself

I'm quite certain you spend a fair amount of time thinking about your faults and all those things you have done wrong, but I wonder how often you remind yourself just how good a person you are. This has nothing at all to do with being vain or over-confident. It is a case of being realistic. There is an old adage that 'If you don't love yourself, how can you expect anyone else to do so?' Just think about that for a moment. Imagine that you are faced with two people, each of whom would like to spend some time with you. One person really looks miserable. 'I don't suppose you fancy coming for a walk . . .?' they say. 'You're probably far too busy and I expect it will rain anyway. I'm sorry to have bothered you.'

'It's such a beautiful day,' the other one says. 'Let's go for a walk. It's ages since we had the chance to talk and I'd love to hear what's going on in your life at the moment.' The expression on the second person's smiling face tells you that she really means what she is saying.

Which of those two people would you feel more like spending an hour of your time with – the one who is miserable from the outset or the one who looks and sounds as if she really wants to share the beautiful day with you? I know which I would choose.

When working with individual patients on a course of therapy, one of the tasks I often set them is to make a list of all those things about themselves that they like and another of all those things they do not like. (This applies to personality traits rather than to colour of eyes, size of feet etc.) No one has any trouble compiling a list of dislikes and this one is always far longer than the list of those things they like and appreciate about themselves.

Why not try making just the positive list about yourself? Do it now. Stop reading, find a pen and paper, and take the time to write down everything you can think of about yourself that you like. And remember, I am not asking you to list what you have *achieved* but what you *like* – not the same thing at all. You may never have passed an exam, reached the top of your chosen tree, been asked out by the most attractive man or woman in the town, or won the London Marathon. But you might be kind, loving, sincere, honest and a hard worker. See just how long you can make that list.

When you have completed your list, read it through several times. Can anyone who has all those positive qualities really be such a bad person? I think not. Pin the list up on the wall or fix it to a cupboard door. Look at it often and realise that you really are a terrific person.

— *The words you say to yourself* —

In the beginning your low self-esteem was probably created to a great extent by other people. If, when you were a child, a parent, teacher or other adult told you that you were 'hopeless', 'stupid' or 'would never amount to anything', you would have accepted it. After all, when we are little, we think grown-ups know everything, don't we? The strange thing is that, even when we are adults ourselves, and can see and understand the fallibility of our former critics with our logical minds, the subconscious still clings to the impression originally created and we never progress far from those negative thoughts.

This being the case, it takes only a few words from an unkind person to bring all that old negativity to the fore. Only this time the real harm is done by the internal words you say to yourself once the other person has finished speaking.

Suppose, for example, I came to you and said 'Your hair looks dreadful; it has just turned bright blue'. I don't suppose that would worry you at all. It certainly wouldn't lower your self-esteem. Why is this? Well you *know* for a fact that your hair hasn't turned bright blue so the words you would say (or think) to yourself once I had finished speaking would be along the lines of 'Silly fool. What is she thinking of? My hair is the same colour as it always was.' And your self-esteem would remain at its former level.

Suppose, however, I said to you 'I know what that terrible thing was you did in the past' – how would you feel then? Because none of us is a saint and because we have all made mistakes in the past or done things which caused us to feel foolish or guilty, you would immediately think of whichever event you feel most badly about. Your internal conversation might run 'Oh no, she knows about it. How did she find out? Is she going to tell anyone? I wish it had never happened.' You would now be feeling far more negative and your self-esteem would have plummeted.

In neither of those examples did your self-esteem suffer because of *my* words. The damage was done by what you thought after I had finished speaking. And this is always the case. So there is one very important point to remember:

NO ONE CAN MAKE YOU FEEL INFERIOR WITHOUT YOUR HELP.

Bearing that phrase in mind, if you are feeling inferior because you do not have a job, you are doing it to yourself. Look back at the list of positive aspects of your personality you wrote earlier. Does the fact that you do not have a job change any of those characteristics? Are you now insincere when before you were sincere? Have you changed from being someone who is kind to animals to someone who goes around kicking cats? Have you ceased to be a loving person? Of course not. Your basic personality has not changed. If you are now feeling inferior it is because the way in which you speak to yourself is causing you to do so.

Of course there are unthinking individuals who might consider you less of a person because you have no job. But this is *their* problem. The fact that they think it does not make it so – only you can do that. And should you really be allowing the views of someone so insensitive to colour your life and your well-being.

Repetition and action

There are two essential stages you must undergo if you want to change anything about yourself. One is repetition and the other is action.

If you want to fix something in your mind you have to repeat it frequently – certainly in the initial stages. Have you ever looked up a telephone number and then repeated it to yourself over and over again until you have dialled it? Suppose, however, you needed to call that same number again the following day; you probably had to look it up all over again. Now consider those telephone numbers you call regularly. You may have consulted your address book frequently at the outset, but you have now repeated them so often that they are probably fixed permanently in your mind and you probably don't have to look them up at all.

Try this exercise: say the following phrase to yourself several times each day for the next three weeks:

NO ONE CAN MAKE ME FEEL INFERIOR
WITHOUT MY HELP.

After three weeks the phrase will have become fixed in your subconscious mind so that you will not forget it. After that, any time you find your self-esteem plummeting, repeat the phrase to yourself – aloud if possible. I think you will be pleasantly surprised at the difference it makes.

The other important stage is taking action. Whether you are planning to change your mental outlook or your physical ability, just thinking about it is not enough. If you wanted to learn to roller skate you would have to do more than think about it. You would have to practise it to find out how it feels and what the difficulties are. In the course of this book you are going to find various positive steps you can take to improve your life while you are without a job – and some which may help you to attain one. If you wish, you can simply sit in your armchair and read the book from cover to cover – but will you be any different at the end of it? Or you could select those steps which you feel most apply to you and try putting them into practice, thus making actual changes in yourself in the process. Simply doing this will bring about a sense of achievement and this in turn automatically raises your level of self-esteem.

——— *Overcoming past voices* ———

We have seen how a low opinion of yourself can be created in the first place by the words or actions of others. Because the effect of such words and actions can be deep and long lasting, it is a good idea to spend some time deliberately recalling them and understanding their on-going effects.

There are, of course, instances where the harm has been done deliberately. It is a sad fact that some people are only able to feel strong and powerful if they inflict pain on others – whether that pain is physical or emotional. If you suffered as a child from the words or deeds of such an adult, you may have spent a great part of your life trying to forget. Indeed, in those cases where the pain has been most traumatic, the mind will often block out the most distressing times.

I'm a terrific person!

In other cases the damage will not have been deliberate at all. Perhaps an unthinking adult really believed it would be possible to spur the child on to greater things by means of goading, belittling or even beating. The harm done at the time will have been just as great, but when you come to look back at it from a distance you may be able to see that there was less malice intended.

If these things happened to you many years ago, there is little point in going to the original perpetrator and telling them of the pain they caused (indeed some may not still be alive). If the intention was to cause distress, they are unlikely to feel remorse and, if it was unthinking, they will probably not believe you.

There is, however, a highly effective technique for dealing with this situation and this is described step by step below.

1 Sit quietly and comfortably where you will not be disturbed.

2 Close your eyes and spend a few moments relaxing to the best of your ability.

3 Imagine that you are in a cinema looking up at the screen. On it you can see a scene from your childhood – one which caused you distress at the time. Watch the scene unfold until it reaches the point of greatest upset and then 'freeze' the picture.

4 The child that you were may have felt fear, guilt or unhappiness, but was almost certainly unable to demonstrate anger on his or her own behalf. Today you should not have that problem. So, continuing to watch the screen in your imagination, say to the adult shown there exactly what you would like to say on the child's behalf – you can say the words aloud or you may choose to think them to yourself. Be as angry as you need and make sure you leave the adult on the screen in no doubt as to your opinion of what he or she is doing and the harm they are causing.

5 Allow the picture on the screen to change in the way it would have done had someone really come along and said those words on your behalf at the appropriate time. Think how differently the adult would have acted and how much better you would have felt as a child to know that there was someone speaking up for you.

6 Now let the picture fade. Spend a few moments relaxing and reminding yourself that the effect of that past incident can never again have the effect on you that it had in the past.

If you have many such childhood incidents in mind, you can repeat this process as often as you wish, but it is important only to deal with one situation at a time.

Failure

No one is a saint or in possession of superhuman qualities – so we have all failed at many things in our lives. That is not important. What is important is the way in which you allow those past failures to affect your present life and your current image of yourself.

Perhaps you did not pass all the exams you sat; or perhaps you never quite managed to please an over-ambitious parent. Possibly you have a broken marriage or relationship behind you; or it may be that you did not succeed in being selected for the first team in your chosen sport. The list of possibilities is endless, but let us just take a look at the four examples I gave above.

1 Does failing an exam really make you a bad person? Even if you know that you could have done better had you worked harder, reaching an insufficient level in a particular subject is not the end of the world. Of course it is a blow to the pride and,

should the particular exam be an essential step in your pursuit of a specific career, you may have had to resit it. But you will have learned something from the exercise – that you did not put in enough effort, that your knowledge of the subject in question was less than you believed or that you needed to work on the state of your nerves when taking exams.

2 We have already seen that parents – perhaps unwittingly – can cause a lowering of self-esteem. Think back to your childhood. Do any of these phrases strike a chord: 'You'll never be any good at maths (or languages or music . . .)'; 'Why can't you do as well as your sister?'; 'You weren't trying'; 'You've let me down'? The person you are now should realise that these and similar phrases are unfair and hurtful to a child and therefore the fault lies with the parent rather than with you. I even heard of a case recently where a teenage girl had worked extremely hard to come second in her end-of-year exams. Delighted, she ran home to tell her parents only to have her father tell her that, had she worked even harder, she might have come first.

3 Of course it hurts when relationships go wrong. And, of course, there is a tendency to look back and think 'if only . . .'. But it is hardly ever the case that all blame lies with one partner only – although sometimes the other person will try to convince you this is so. And, if you are someone whose self-esteem is already low, you may well believe what is said to you and allow yourself to take full responsibility. However, there should be some good memories from the time before the relationship began to sour and you will hopefully have learned something from the relationship itself – either that you need to be more careful in your choice of partner or that you need to act differently in some way. It is a sad fact that many relationships do break down, but it is also a fact that most people find themselves able to form subsequent – and frequently happier – attachments.

4 Failing to gain a place on a team can be very demoralising, particularly as you probably made great efforts to be selected.

It can be a great blow to the self-esteem because it feels like a personal rejection rather than a cool appraisal of your skills in a particular field. It doesn't matter if you know that only 7 (or 11 or 15) people can be selected and that 23 were trying, being turned down still hurts.

There are two ways of regarding moments of failure; you can either see them as learning experiences or you can take them as reinforcement of your inner belief that you are no good. And yet, even those whom one feels should not make mistakes do so. I am positive that there is no great diva of the opera who has never missed a note; I have seen the world's greatest tennis players serve a series of double faults; champion skaters have been known to slip and fall on the ice. If all those people can pick themselves up from (often public) mistakes and go on, surely we should be able to do the same?

You used to be able to do that. When you were a tiny child learning to walk you must have fallen over time and time again. But presumably you persevered or you would still be crawling around on all fours. If you could overcome your failures at a year old, you must be able to do as well today.

Feeling guilty

Have you done something in the past which you now regret – or perhaps feel guilty because you failed to act or speak in a particular way on some occasion? You are not alone. There is no one who cannot find some moment in their past which they would change if only they could.

You can choose to allow these feelings of guilt to lower your self-esteem and therefore affect you for the rest of your life. Or you can take the following steps:

- apologise if you were in the wrong and this is still possible;

- do what you can to make amends if this is still appropriate;

- resolve to act differently in the future.

Once you have done all that, there is no point at all in concentrating on the past and your feelings of guilt. If you do not want it to affect your present and your future, you must learn your lesson and let it go.

——————— *Compliments* ———————

Most of us are very bad at giving and receiving compliments. Somehow we seem to find it easier to criticise – whether ourselves or other people. And yet both paying and receiving compliments can be a great boost to the self-esteem.

If you pay someone else a genuine compliment – even if they are diffident in the way they accept it – you are making them feel better. It is always good to know that someone appreciates you or what you do. If someone compliments you, even if you feel embarrassed at the time, you will still feel a glow, knowing that you are considered worthy of the compliment. This is a win/win situation with both parties receiving a boost to their self-esteem.

Many people do feel embarrassed and do not know what to say when being paid a compliment. You must have heard an exchange like this:

> *'I do like your outfit; it really suits you.'*
> *'Oh, this old thing; I've had it for years.'*

Now you have a lose/lose situation. The person to whom the compliment was paid is probably furious with him or herself for

——— 35 ———

being so ungracious to someone who was being generous, while the person who paid the compliment, instead of feeling happy for boosting someone else, now feels deflated by the response. In fact, in the example given, it is almost like saying 'your judgement is no good' which is a blow to the self-esteem.

If you tend to find yourself lost for words when complimented, all you need do is smile and say 'Thank you', and everyone will feel happy.

Why not make a real effort to look for ways in which to pay other people compliments in the coming week? I am not talking about telling lies for the sake of it – there is nothing more obvious than the obviously false 'darling you look *wonderful*' type of statement. But a simple 'That was a delicious meal' or 'I'm very proud of you' can do wonders for both parties.

— *The importance of boosting* — *your self-esteem*

Why is it so important to do all that you can to boost your self-esteem? Well, unless you are a recluse living in a cave in a hillside, you are going to come into contact with many other people in the course of your daily life and a negative person is so depressing to be around. Friends and family may love you dearly and may sympathise with the position in which you find yourself – but continue to be negative and you will find that either they begin to lose patience with you or that they start to avoid you altogether.

In the same way, until you are feeling confident that you have improved your self-image, you would probably do well to keep away from other negative people. When you are feeling down, the last thing you need is to be reminded of the number of unemployed, the recession or the catalogue of disasters in another individual's personal life.

There was an old music-hall song about a man who felt fine until everyone he met started telling him how ill he looked. He was only saved from gloom and despondency by his encounter with a friend who told him he looked wonderful. His actual state of health had not varied from start to finish, but his attitude had been coloured dramatically by the negative words he encountered.

Apart from not wanting to have a depressing effect on your friends and family, you may be in a position where you will be asked to attend a job interview. You are not going to make a very good impression, however wonderful your qualifications, if you come across as someone with a low opinion of yourself. And a well-trained interviewer will soon be able to pick this up. No one wants to employ someone so negative that he or she may well have a depressing effect on other members of staff, so, although I am not suggesting you should portray yourself as vain or superior, an air of quiet confidence and belief in yourself can make all the difference in an interview. And, although this air of confidence can be assumed even when you do not really feel it, it is far more convincing if you *do* believe in yourself.

Someone with high self-esteem is usually an achiever because they are willing to take risks and try something new. Of course not everything will turn out to be a success but, if you do not try, you will never know. So take every realistic opportunity offered to you; you never know where it will lead and you might enjoy yourself along the way.

Dale Carnegie uses a saying in his books and courses: 'Act enthusiastic and you'll be enthusiastic'. And it really works – try it for yourself. In fact, there is one large corporation in the US where the boss will often approach an employee and ask how he or she is doing. If the answer is anything other than 'Terrific!', the hapless employee is fined the sum of $50. Whether you approve of this approach or not, that particular organisation has an enthusiastic work force and an extremely high productivity rate.

EFFECT OF SELF-ESTEEM ON PHYSICAL AND MENTAL HEALTH

Although an isolated temporary set-back or a single day when you may not be feeling on top of the world will make no difference at all to your physical or mental well-being, a prolonged period of low self-esteem can certainly do so. Those who are not at ease with themselves as people soon begin to display all the symptoms of stress and, of course, the longer these symptoms continue the greater the draining effect on the self-esteem.

Henry was a typical example of this pattern. Due to the Victorian attitudes of his authoritarian father, he had never had a great deal of confidence in himself. Nor had he dared to be ambitious, believing that he was incapable of achieving anything more than the mundane. He had gone to work as a young apprentice in a large manufacturing company in the south of England. His apprenticeship over, he had worked steadily and hard for the same organisation for nearly 30 years. He had never sought to further himself and had, in fact, refused promotion to the position of works supervisor when it was offered, preferring to stay with what he knew he could do, rather than take the chance of failing at a higher level.

Then the recession struck. The company was compelled to reduce its work force and Henry feared that, at 49 years of age, he was about to find himself on the redundancy list. His father's words still ringing in his subconscious ears, he did not think to himself 'I am a hard and conscientious worker and I have been with the company since my apprenticeship'. His self-esteem was so low that he assumed the firm would want to be rid of him as soon as possible. He began to get headaches and soon found himself unable to sleep at night. The longer the situation dragged on, the lower his self-esteem became and the more obvious his symptoms. His appetite disappeared and he even had one or two panic attacks.

Originally those in charge of the company had no intention of making Henry redundant. They appreciated the work he had done over the years – and it would also have cost them quite a lot of money! But, as his symptoms developed, his work deteriorated until the time came when they were quite relieved to let him go. Of course, Henry could now tell himself that he had been right all along, that he was unwanted and useless, and so his self-esteem plunged even lower.

By the time he actually left work, Henry had done such a splendid job of convincing himself that he was a poor risk as a worker that it never occured to him to apply for any other jobs or even to do something positive with his free time. He had made up his mind that no one would want him so what was the point of trying?

Now Henry had even more time to worry and to think, and he grew ever more depressed. He had devoted his life to his work, always being there to do overtime when asked, and so he had never acquired any outside hobbies and interests. He didn't seem to have the energy to do so now – and he didn't see the point. He felt his useful life was over. At 49 years old! He cut himself off from bewildered friends and family, having convinced himself that they would want nothing to do with a failure like him.

Fortunately for Henry, he had one determined friend who refused to be pushed aside and spent a great deal of time talking to him – even though in the beginning he did not really want to listen. Eventually this friend convinced Henry that he was liked for himself and gradually – very gradually – he began the slow climb back to some measure of self-esteem. But for that one friend he could easily have become severely depressed or ill – or both.

Achievement list

One of the things you might find helpful if you find it difficult to believe that you are a terrific person is to create an achievement list. Whoever you are and whatever you have done with your life, you will have things to put on that list. You are an achiever. After all, as a baby you learned to walk didn't you? That's quite an achievement. And, from being an infant with no understanding of words at all, you can now speak and write a whole language. That's an achievement too. If you were an under-achiever, you would still be lying on your back making baby noises.

To make an achievement list, divide your life so far into three. So, if you are 60 years old now, each section would cover 20 years. If you are thirty, a section would cover 10 years. In each section, write down at least four things you achieved during that period.

Before you claim that you have 'never achieved anything in your life', these do not have to be great or world-shaking events. Perhaps at one stage you learned to swim; in another you may have passed your driving test. Perhaps you decorated a room; or successfully grew your own vegetables. Each of these is an achievement and something to be proud of. The problem is that most people, while only too willing to spend time concentrating on those things they have done wrong or missed out on, very rarely work on listing the things they have managed to do.

Your achievement list has nothing to do with vanity. It is an honest chronicle of your abilities. And, although I have encountered many people who have claimed initially that they did not have any real achievements to write down, I can assure you that, after some gentle probing on my part, there was not one who could not find more than four for each section. I have no reason to believe that you would be any different.

When your list is complete, put it in some obvious place so that you can look at it often, and remind yourself that you are a special person with special talents and abilities.

—— *Break the negative spiral* ——

People with low self-esteem will often react to a suggestion with 'I can't . . .' If you say this often enough you will soon believe it.

There is an Eastern saying which claims 'We are what we think, having become what we thought' – in other words, if you think you are no good at something, you are no good at it. Henry Ford said much the same when he claimed that: 'If you think you can or you think you can't – you're right'.

It is possible, however, to break that negative spiral. If you catch yourself saying such things as 'I can't (change a plug)' or 'I always (forget names)', try putting 'until now' in front of it. 'Until now I didn't know how to change a plug' or 'Until now I have always forgotten people's names'. This is only a small difference, yet by speaking in this way you will be convincing your subconscious mind that things are going to be different in the future. You cannot change what you were or what you did in the past but, so far as the future is concerned, you have a choice. You may *choose* never to learn how to change a plug, but that will not lower your self-esteem. Taking the attitude that you must be useless because it is something everyone else can do certainly will.

Affirmations

Whether written or spoken, affirmations can be very useful tools when it comes to improving your self-image. From the days of Emil Coué when it became fashionable to walk about saying 'Every day and in every way I'm growing better and better', people with a positive outlook have been using affirmations to increase their confidence.

Affirmations can be used in general or specific situations. The student facing exams might tell himself 'I will pass; I will succeed', while the person with a low self-esteem might choose to convince her subconscious 'I am an achiever; I am a special person'. I am not claiming for a moment that affirmations are all it takes. No student will pass his exams if he does not study; but many who have revised still fail because they do not believe they have the ability to pass – and this is where the affirmations can make all the difference.

There are two effective ways of using affirmations and you might care to try both until you find which you prefer.

- *Spoken affirmations*   Coué believed that the phrase should be repeated 20 times in succession and, to prevent the train of thought being broken by the need to count, he suggested trying 20 knots in a piece of string and repeating the phrase once for each knot.

- *Written affirmations*   Write the affirmations on several pieces of paper and fix these up in places you have to look – the bathroom mirror, the door of the refrigerator. Even though, once you have grown used to the fact that they are there, you may not actually consciously stop to read what is on the paper, your subconscious will certainly be aware of it. And it is your subconscious mind we are trying to work on, for it is there that all those words and images from the past are firmly entrenched.

Visualisation

If affirmations are a way of using words to alter your inner view of yourself, visualisation does the same thing by means of images.

For visualisation to be effective you need a specific situation rather than an abstract concept. Then you go through the following procedure.

1 Sit in a place where you will be undisturbed. Close your eyes and spend a few moments relaxing as much as possible.

2 Picture yourself in the particular situation you have chosen, imagining everything happening just as you would dearly like it to. It is a little like being the screenplay writer, director and leading actor in a film of part of your own life. You can choose exactly how you would like everything to be.

3 Play through the scene in your mind remembering to *see* the image and also to *feel* what it would be like for everything to happen as you have chosen to visualise it. It is important that you believe in the image you have chosen.

4 Repeat this process daily for at least three weeks. It takes approximately this length of time to convince the sub-conscious mind of the reality of the new images. But you will find that, after this time, your inner perception of yourself will really begin to change. The one really important point to bear in mind is that your subconscious cannot tell the difference between what is real and what is imagined. Until now it has been working on whatever negative data have been fed into it during the course of your life. Now it will come to accept the positive information as reality and will cause you to feel more positive about yourself as a result.

Steps to a higher level of self-esteem

Because this is such an important section of the book, what follows is a step-by-step technique which, if you work through it, will enable you to raise the level of your own self-esteem and to believe in yourself as the terrific person you really are.

- *Think about yourself* Don't just remind yourself of your bad points; concentrate on all those good ones. Make a list of all the good qualities you possess and read it often.

- *Think about your early life* Can you recall who it was who first caused you to feel inferior? Remind yourself that they were wrong to do so (even if their motives were good), because it is an unfair way to behave towards a child.

- *The words you say to yourself* Now that you are adult, it is not the words spoken by another person which have this demoralising effect on you, but the words you say to yourself after they have finished speaking. Remember – no one can make you feel inferior without your help.

- *Repetition and action* Both of these are essential if you are to make changes in yourself. Repeat regularly for three weeks NO ONE CAN MAKE ME FEEL INFERIOR WITHOUT MY HELP and you will be ready to take action towards improving your life.

- *Overcoming past voices* If, as a child, you were unable to react to the unthinking or uncaring adult, practise the technique, described in detail above, of seeing a past event on a large cinema screen in your mind, and then stopping the picture and interceding on behalf of the child you once were.

- *Failure* Remember that there is an enormous difference between having failed at something and being a failure. You may have made mistakes, but that does *not* make you a failure as a person.

- *Guilt* Guilt is a pointless emotion as it changes nothing. If you have done something wrong in the past, all you can do is make amends where possible, learn from it and resolve never to do it again. Then let it go.

- *Compliments* Make a habit of paying genuine compliments as both parties will then feel good about themselves – a win/win situation. Learn to accept compliments graciously; a simple 'thank you' is all that is needed.

- *Negative people* Until you have raised the level of your self-esteem you would do well to keep away from negative people. Similarly, if you allow yourself to become negative, you will find others trying to avoid you.

- *Physical and mental well-being* Low self-esteem can have a detrimental effect on your physical and mental health, and, since this will cause your esteem to drop still further, you will be embarking on a downward spiral from which it may be very difficult to break free.

- *Achievements* You are an achiever and have been from the day you learned to walk. Create an achievement list for your life so far and refer to it often.

- *Break the negative spiral* Change 'I can't . . .' to 'Until now I wasn't able to . . .'.

- *Affirmations* Make use of spoken and written affirmations. Repeat the former 20 times in succession and place the latter in prominent positions so that your subconscious mind is aware of them as you go about your daily tasks.

- *Visualisation* Use visual images to convince your subconscious mind that you are going to achieve whatever you wish. Repeat them daily for three weeks to fix them in your subconscious. Always see a positive outcome.

- *Important phrases:*
  'If you think you can or you think you can't – you're right.'
  'No one can make you feel inferior without your help.'
  'We are what we think having become what we thought.'
  'Act enthusiastic and you'll be enthusiastic.'
  'You're a terrific person!'

4

People matter

There is a great tendency among those who feel depressed or unhappy to cut themselves off from other people. Yet this is the worst thing you can do. If you are to survive and flourish even without a job, you need people now more than ever.

Going to work does more than simply bring in the money to pay the bills. It brings you into contact with other people and allows you to interact with a myriad of personality types. And these people are often the mirror through which we see ourselves. Very few of us take the time for in-depth self-analysis. Our opinion of ourselves is formed largely by the way in which we are treated by others. People who know they are liked and respected by those around them probably quite like themselves while those who – even if they do not care to admit it to themselves – realise that others go out of their way to avoid them or are, at best, coldly civil *know* in their inner selves that they are doing something wrong. Whether or not they choose to change their personality is a matter of their choice.

Take away all this opportunity for feedback and interaction, and the individual is left with only their own thoughts and emotions for company. This is a difficult situation in which to find yourself at the best of times but, if you are already despondent because you are without a job, your thoughts are likely to be negative ones and, without other people to help bring you out of it, you could easily find yourself trapped on a downward spiral of depression.

Donna found herself in just such a position. A single mother in her mid-20s, she enjoyed her work in the cosmetics section of a large department store. The work was pleasant, she loved being among the delightfully perfumed packages containing the products of a leading manufacturer of beauty preparations and the salary, although not extremely high, was sufficient to keep her and her daughter, and to pay for a child-minder when three-year-old Kerry came home from nursery school. But to Donna the most important aspect of her work was the company of the other young women in the department. Much as she loved Kerry, the conversation of a three-year-old child is somewhat limited and, as she usually stayed at home in the evenings, she would otherwise have had quite a lonely existence.

Then came the cut-backs and, along with several others on the cosmetics floor, Donna suddenly found herself without a job. As a single parent she was entitled to various financial benefits and these enabled her to pay all the basic bills, but certainly did not provide sufficient funds for a child-minder. Nor was there now any need for one as Donna could no longer afford the fees of the nursery school, or to go out with or without her daughter.

At first the other girls from the store – some of whom still worked there and some of whom had also lost their jobs – tried to keep in touch with Donna. They would telephone to see how she was or ask her to their homes for coffee. But Donna refused all invitations. She felt it would be too difficult to go everywhere with a small child and, in her depressed state, she convinced herself that the others were being patronising and condescending, and were only approaching her out of pity.

Soon the only outings Donna made were her weekly trips to the local supermarket. She became more and more withdrawn until she hardly even bothered to communicate with Kerry, preferring to leave it to television programmes to keep her daughter company. Not understanding why her mother had changed in this way, Kerry became difficult and demanding, and this, of course, only added to Donna's sense of hopelessness. She began to dislike herself more and more until she believed that not only was she so useless at her job that the company had been glad to get rid of her, but that she was a terrible mother too, unable to cope with one three-year-old little girl.

If, however, Donna had responded to those early contacts from her former colleagues, think how different the situation might have been. She would have had the pleasure of the company of other young women of her own age – people she already knew and liked, and who obviously liked her or they would not have bothered to issue invitations in the first place. They would not have had to do anything which cost a great deal of money – after all, some of the others found themselves in a similar situation to Donna. A cup of coffee in a friend's home, an afternoon in the local park – these things cost little or nothing but can be very pleasurable.

Donna's self-esteem, instead of plunging to the depths, would have been raised, and she would have found herself being more patient and communicative with Kerry. She might even have found that, by maintaining contact with her friends, she was able to learn of another job for which she could apply and so return to her former, happier situation.

If you find yourself without a job and not enjoying the situation, the first people to talk to are those nearest to you – your immediate family or your closest friends. Anyone who cares about you will have time to listen, will care and will be willing to help wherever possible. No one who has your interests at heart is going to think any less of you for finding yourself in a difficult current situation. So talk to them, tell them what has happened and how it makes you feel – and listen to what they say to you. They may not be able to offer much in the way of practical help in finding work, but use them as your 'mirror' and let them help you to maintain a reasonably high opinion of yourself.

Some people keep things to themselves for what they consider to be the best possible reasons. When Martin knew that redundancy was a possibility, he said nothing at all to his wife because he did not want to cause her worry. When the axe finally fell he did not know how to tell her. And so, for about five weeks, he lived a lie. Every morning he would set off as if to go to the office, returning home at the usual time in the evening. During the day he would drift from one coffee shop to another, reading innumerable newspapers, and drinking endless cups of tea and coffee.

Martin's wife, not being a fool, guessed that something was wrong, but had no idea at all what it could be. She knew her husband had changed drastically and she felt that he was not being honest with her. The only thing she could think of was that he no longer loved her or that he was having an affair. After agonising about the situation for some days, she felt that she had to know the truth and confronted Martin on his return one evening.

Martin couldn't believe what he was hearing. It had not occurred to him that his wife had noticed any difference in him and certainly not that she would suspect him of being unfaithful to her. He immediately told her the truth about the situation, expecting her to be relieved. In fact she was furious that he had not trusted her sufficiently to let her know what was happening and that he had not believed her capable of dealing with the situation, while still continuing to care for him and respect him.

It was fortunate that Martin and his wife had a strong, loving relationship because it was now being drastically strained. A weaker marriage might well have foundered but, although it took them a while to sort out their differences, this particular couple eventually became closer and therefore a stronger unit.

If you find your income reduced because you do not have a job, your family and close friends deserve to know this too. Many people try to keep up appearances, only to find themselves under greater and greater pressure as time goes by. Of course we would all like to continue our former lifestyle and to give those we care for the things we have always given them. But sometimes this is just not possible and it is better by far to talk about this at the outset, and decide together what can and cannot be done. Careful joint budgeting might still leave money for occasional treats – and there are lots of things you can do which do not have to cost much. You don't have to invite friends for a meal; real friends come to see you, not to eat your food, so they will be just as happy with a cup of coffee.

You may find it difficult to maintain contact with former work fellows – perhaps you never really got on well with them, you may have given up work some time ago or possibly you have never had a job. This does not mean you have to condemn yourself to an isolated life. If you are fit enough to be out and about, there are all sorts of things you can do.

Do you have an interest or a hobby? Then find a group or organisation near you (your local library should have details of addresses and contact numbers) which is devoted to that particular interest. Many of these groups are inexpensive to join and you can be sure that you will have something in common with those you meet there. A glance at the noticeboard in my library shows that there are organisations specialising in all manner of interests – astrology, discussion, walking, gardening, local history, the list is endless.

Even if you are a beginner in your chosen subject, don't feel that you cannot go along. You will find any number of 'experts' only too happy to give you friendly advice and information. In fact, if you are someone who usually finds breaking the ice difficult, you might even decide to pretend to know less than you do as a means of starting a conversation.

Another really positive aspect of such groups is that they contain people from a broad spectrum of life rather than all retired, all unemployed, all student etc. There is nothing wrong, of course, with going along to these groups too; you will still have something in common with all the others there which is a good starting point for communication. Just be sure that you don't allow yourself to become involved in the depressing 'Isn't life terrible' sort of conversation each time you go or you will end up feeling more negative than at the outset.

Adult education classes can provide another interesting way of meeting new people while teaching you a new skill at the same time. And such classes are usually very inexpensive for the unemployed or retired. Whether you want to learn car maintenance, a foreign language or clay modelling, every area offers a variety of subjects both at day and evening classes. Here, too, you will automatically have something in common with everyone you meet and there is usually a break in the middle of the session, giving you time to become better acquainted and to talk informally.

In addition to providing you with an interesting way of spending your time and meeting new people, such classes may well provide you with a new set of skills which you can put to good money-making use in the future.

If you are actually looking for employment, as opposed to having retired, any one of those new people you meet could turn out to be just the contact you need. The old saying that 'It's not what you know – it's who you know' is often true. The more people who are aware of your situation the better, because one of them might come to know of an opportunity which would suit you and, if they have already come to know you, might well be willing to mention you to the appropriate person.

Take the example of Steven. He had never had a job. He left school at 18 after taking his A levels which he passed with grades which were too low to allow him to go to university. Keen to begin his working life, he set out with enthusiasm to look for work – only to find that every door seemed to be closed to him. When, in desperation, he began to apply for low-paid menial jobs, he found that he was even turned down for these – 'You're over-qualified' he was told.

Even with all the job applications he was writing, Steven found that he had an excess of time on his hands and he decided to put it to good use by learning something new. Studying the lists of subjects offered at his local adult education college, he decided to join two classes – one in car maintenance which he thought would prove useful and one in watercolour painting as this was something he had always wanted to try.

There were 18 people in the watercolour class, and they were of all ages and from all walks of life. As the term progressed the class members would assemble in groups at coffee time and chat. Steven became friendly with Susan Parsons, a woman in her late 40s to whom he found it easy to speak. He told her about his quest for a job and how it had so far proved to be fruitless. The following week Mrs Parsons told him that she had been speaking to her husband who ran his own small company and who was looking for a new clerical assistant. She had told him about Steven and Mr Parsons said that, if he wished to apply for the job, he would be happy to interview him. He did so the following week and Steven was able at last to join the ranks of the employed. All this was because he decided to make full use of his time by learning a new skill.

If you are actively seeking a job, networking can prove to be extremely beneficial. There is a great tendency – whatever your common sense tells you about the situation – to feel ashamed of being unemployed, and to try and hide the fact from people you meet. But you might be doing yourself a great disservice and missing opportunities which might present themselves to you.

Rather than trying to hide the facts, let everyone know that you are looking for work, and what your skills and abilities are. You do not have to go on and on about it as it would soon become boring, and you might even find people trying to avoid you. But do make sure that as many people as possible know of your situation, as you can never tell from which direction an opportunity might come.

Joining groups and meeting new people is also a good idea for those who are retired. There are innumerable possibilities. Some groups and organisations exist solely for those of retirement age, while others are more general and cater for all ages. If you have the time, why not try both? Of course it is pleasant to mix with others of your own age and situation, but there is much to be said for interactive communication between the generations, and many a senior citizen has found that mixing with people younger than themselves has kept them young and alert in outlook.

Even if you are lucky enough still to have your partner with you, it is as well to do some things individually. However much you love someone and enjoy their company, it is not really healthy to spend 24 hours a day with them. For one thing, it is easy to become irritated by each other and, for another, you will have far more to talk about if you each have private interests. This was part of the thinking behind the main Probus groups for retired business and professional people which have sprung up over the past few years. These are separated into men's and women's groups, and each have meetings with speakers on a vast variety of topics giving those with partners plenty to talk about when they get back together.

Without wishing to be morbid or depressing, another reason for having separate interests is that there is always the possibility that one partner might find him or herself left alone. If you have always done everything together you will find it extremely difficult to *start* finding new outlets at such a time. But, if you have always had people who have known you as an individual rather than as half of a partnership, these people could prove to be your greatest support when you need them.

Ellen and Alfred had been married for 52 years when Alfred died quite suddenly. Until that time they had always done everything and been everywhere together. In fact Ellen always used to boast that they did not need anyone else; they had each other, their daughter and their three delightful grandchildren.

After Alfred's death, their daughter Vera spent a lot of time with her mother, bringing the grandchildren to visit whenever she could and inviting Ellen to stay with them at regular intervals. About two years later, however, Vera came to her mother with the news that her husband Bill had been offered a wonderful job in Boston, in the US – too good to consider turning down. A beautiful home went with the job, the money was excellent and they would be able to offer their children so much more than they would if they stayed in the UK. She hoped her mother would understand that they had no alternative – they really had to accept the offer for the sake of their whole family.

Ellen was devastated. She hardly heard Vera telling her that she would be welcome to visit them as often as she wished, staying for as long as she liked. All she could think of was how empty her world was going to be. Her family had always been everything to her; so much so that she had never really made any friends but was just on casual 'Good morning' terms with her neighbours.

If you find yourself suddenly left alone at Ellen's age, it is very difficult to venture out into the world, develop new interests and form new friendships. So, although maintaining your own interests and friends should not be looked on simply as an insurance policy against loneliness, it can make all the difference to the way you feel if you do find yourself alone in later life.

This is also the reason why people should think long and hard before moving to a strange area as soon as they retire. It is lovely to think of spending your time on a balcony in Spain or in a cottage by the sea, but you also have to take into account that as you grow older you often need the familiarity of well-loved surroundings or good friends, particularly should ill-health or bereavement occur. Of course it is possible for such problems to confront anyone of any age but – although in these days most people live a longer active life – the likelihood is often greater in later years.

Of course this is not to say that retiring to some distant idyllic spot cannot be a wonderful experience, bringing with it a new lease of life. It can prove to be a happy and fulfilling time – a dream come true. But it is not something to be rushed into without careful thought about possible future events.

There are some people who, because of domestic ties, poor health or disability, find themselves unable to leave the confines of their home for more than essential trips. For such people it would obviously be difficult to join a group or organisation which entailed making a commitment to be in a certain place on regular dates. But this does not mean that there is no way of keeping in touch with other people or even of making new friends.

Many housebound and disabled people seem to have discovered the knack of being such good company, in spite of their problems, that others are only too eager to come and spend time with them. The positive attitude of such people makes them a joy to be with at any time.

There are others, however, who allow their thoughts to turn inwards, and who become so negative and depressing that their only visitors are those who come out of pity. Of course it is easy to understand how such a situation can arise, but in the long run they hurt themselves far more than anyone else and in the end they contribute to their own loneliness.

One of the liveliest and most positive people I knew was a woman who had been paralysed as the result of a riding accident when she was just 20. Until that time she had been a young, active woman who loved to swim, dance and spend time with her horses. By the time I met her she was nearly 40 and so had spent about half her life in a wheelchair. She told me that, immediately after the accident, she had become withdrawn and bitter, and wanted to die. And then she realised that her attitude was causing her friends to avoid coming to see her or, when pity drew them to her side, they stayed as short a time as possible before making excuses to leave.

At that point she was faced with a choice; she could either continue to be bitter about a situation she was unable to change and risk losing all her friends or she could try to find as many aspects of life as possible which still gave her pleasure. Fortunately she chose the latter course and soon her friends came to see her, not out of any sense of duty but because she was fun to be with.

If you find yourself stuck at home – whatever the reason – you could consider becoming a penfriend. You might not be able to travel to far-distant countries, but contact with people who live in them might enable you to know more about the way of life there than is discovered by many two-week tourists. Through letters you can share in the lives of people of all ages and nationalities until you feel you really are part of their extended family. And the fact that you have to tell them something in return will compel you to look around your own world and find interesting things to write about.

Writing letters is a comparatively cheap way of keeping in touch with people – the amount of pleasure you can receive far exceeds the cost of paper and a stamp. If you can afford slightly more, many people nowadays are corresponding by means of spoken cassette, and finding that hearing the voices and sounds from some distant place is an even better way of keeping in touch. The same cassette can be used over and over again, so it is the cost of the postage which is the main consideration.

If you have the time, the inclination and the small amount of money required, you can correspond (whether in writing or on cassette) with several people in your own country or in various parts of the world, thus broadening your knowledge and your interests and widening your circle of friends.

People are important. However much we think we can survive happily without contact with other people, we find we cannot. To understand the many negative results of trying to 'go it alone', have a look at a case history taken from one of my own patient files (the name has obviously been changed).

When Denis was made redundant for the third time in as many years, he became very negative. Now, of course, this was quite understandable as he had just suffered repeated blows to his self-esteem, but it had a devastating effect on his life. From being a man who had always been able to pick himself up and try again, he withdrew completely into his shell. He refused to contemplate looking for another job as he felt if would be pointless saying that 'As soon as things get tough I'll just be made redundant again'.

A single man, he stayed in his bed-sitter day after long day, only going out to cash his unemployment benefit and do any essential shopping. When friends tried to keep in touch he refused to have anything to do with them, eventually becoming so unpleasant to them that they give up trying. His life soon consisted of watching television, smoking and staring at the same four walls.

Eventually, his self-esteem having plunged to the depths. Denis began to dislike himself intensely. Because he had this low opinion of himself, he assumed that everyone else felt this way about him too. They didn't of course – but from his position of self-pity Denis was not observing reality, only what he perceived to be the truth. He began to grow angry – angry with himself for being what he thought of as a 'failure', angry with his friends for disliking him and angry with the world for being such a miserable place.

His friends, on the other hand, did not understand why Denis was cutting himself off in this way. They did not feel dislike or contempt for him – only sorry that he had lost three jobs in a row on a 'last in, first out' basis. Initially they were anxious to maintain contact with him, to include him in their outings and, hopefully, to keep him as cheerful as possible. But it is very hard to help someone who does not want to be helped, and eventually they grew disillusioned and resentful that he was taking his bitterness out on them. They began to leave him alone.

This, of course, convinced Denis that he had been right all along. His so-called 'friends' didn't really care about him after all or they would still be keeping in touch. He didn't stop to think that perhaps it was his attitude – not his lack of a job – which was keeping them away. He became a very lonely man.

By the time I met Denis this situation had been going on for some time. He had reached the stage where his doctor had prescribed a course of anti-depressants which, although helpful in the beginning, were becoming less and less effective as time went on. Not wanting to take anything stronger and realising that he had to do something about putting his life in order before things grew even worse, he finally came to consult me for possible help.

While helping Denis, with the aid of hypnotherapy, gradually to reduce the amount of tablets he was taking, I started to work with him on dealing with the underlying situation – the self-dislike and the reason for it. We discussed the redundancies and I asked Denis whether, if the same thing had happened to one of his friends, he would suddenly dislike them. 'Of course not', he replied.

'So why do you assume they all dislike you?' I asked. He did not answer.

Then I suggested he should consider what it must be like to try and be friendly with someone who was always bitter and morose, and who rejected all approaches – how would he feel in such a situation? Denis said it must be very hurtful to find your friendship constantly refused. 'Bearing that in mind,' I said, 'what do you think is the real reason for your friends leaving you alone now?'

For the first time since I had known him, Denis smiled. He was not a fool, just a man who had been so caught up in his own misfortune that he had not been able to see things objectively. All it took was an outsider to put the situation in perspective and he could see that he had been his own worst enemy.

'What are you going to do about it?' I asked. He smiled again. 'Make a few phone calls and a few apologies', he replied.

If you find yourself without a job, the worst thing you can do is cut yourself off from your friends and family. Unless you have made a very poor choice of friends, no one is going to like you any the less because you are not working – and if they did like you less, they would not be worth calling 'friend' anyway. Should you catch yourself beginning to believe that people are only keeping in touch with you out of pity, stop and ask yourself how you would feel had the positions been reversed. And if you do reach the stage, as Denis did, where the approaches grow less, don't tell yourself that this is proof that all those people never did like you in the first place. Try wondering whether it could possibly have been your attitude which made them feel uncomfortable and unwelcome.

Close family relationships often suffer when one partner becomes unemployed – particularly if that loss of employment came about suddenly. Zelda West-Meads of Relate has said, 'We've had a fifteen per cent increase in couples seeking counselling for each of the years since the recession started.'

Men are often the hardest hit – particularly older men who may have grown up in a time when the man was the 'breadwinner' and his value as a person seemed to be closely linked with his capabilities as a provider. Such men feel angry and ashamed that they are 'letting down' their wives and families. (This is so even when the wives and families are understanding and sympathetic.)

In situations where one partner has a job while the other is desperately seeking one, the latter may feel completely misunderstood. He or she might become angry and even belligerent believing that their partner cannot possibly understand how they are feeling when they are not in the same position themselves. Resentment can also develop on both sides – out of jealousy over employment on the one hand and from the pressure of being the sole provider where formerly there were two incomes on the other.

Such resentment has nothing to do with logic. The person without the job is naturally pleased that their partner has an income while the earner, who would probably not resent being the only provider if the home situation was pleasant, might find it irksome in the extreme to have to support someone whose behaviour and manner are unpleasant.

This whole problem can be made to appear far greater because it is not unusual for someone whose unemployment is causing despondency to lose all sexual desire. This applies to both men and women, and results from a loss of self-esteem, made worse by an inability to discuss feelings and fears. Unless the couple can remain close and loving a severe emotional crisis can result.

If you find yourself having to survive without a job when you would far rather have one – and especially if this has come about suddenly or earlier than you would have wished – there are various phases through which you can expect to pass. The initial sensation is probably one of shock and disbelief – how could this be happening to *you*?

Once the feeling of shock wears off, you can expect to experience sharp swings of mood. You will probably fluctuate between feeling that this is your golden opportunity and the world is a wonderful place, and wallowing in despair and bitterness. It is important to realise that these mood swings are normal and indeed that it is necessary to experience them if you are to emerge whole and strong at the other end of the tunnel. The frame of mind into which you finally settle depends on the way in which you deal with the situation and how positive you are determined to be.

Always remember that you are a very special person – unique in fact. You have talents and abilities, and the fact that you do not have an opportunity to prove this by having a job at the moment is not a slur upon you but a reflection of a situation which happens to exist. Talk to other people, keeping all lines of communication open and you will maintain the ability to see things as they really are, not as they look from the bottom of a well of depression.

Checklist

- Expect changes of mood in the early days. These are normal and will pass.

- Be honest from the outset; don't try and hide your situation.

- Remember that being without a job does not make you a failure as a person – and that no one else is going to see you in that light.

- Talk to friends, to family, to a counsellor if necessary, to possible employers, to former colleagues. Use these people as a 'mirror' to reflect and enhance your own sense of self-worth.

- If you try and keep things to yourself, other people will try to guess what the problem is and may well guess wrongly, thinking that you have some guilty secret to hide. Their behaviour will obviously change – which will confuse you – and misunderstandings will arise all round.

- Don't try to keep up appearances when finances will not allow it. Anyone who likes you only for what you can give them is not worth bothering about.

- Try joining a group or organisation concerned with a subject which interests you. It costs very little and you will meet people with whom you automatically have something in common.

- Avoid negative people as they will only make you feel worse.

- Join an adult education class to meet new people and develop new skills.

- Networking can prove invaluable in helping you find employment, so let as many people as possible know that you are looking for work.

- However strong your relationships, remember that you are an individual too. Develop interests of your own and encourage your partner to do so too; it will make you both more interesting and give you more to talk about.

- If you are unable to get out, consider becoming a penfriend or communicating with others by means of cassettes.

- Don't insult your friends by rejecting any approaches they make or they will soon leave you alone.

- If you are involved in a close relationship, talk honestly to your partner about your feelings – even about feelings of envy if they are working. They will understand and any situation which is understood can be dealt with.

- Expect to experience quite dramatic mood swings in the early days and even a temporary loss of sexual ability. These are *normal* and will pass, provided you do all you can to maintain a positive attitude.

- Should you find yourself becoming withdrawn and bitter, and feeling unable to speak to others, do try and find a qualified counsellor who will be able to help you work through your feelings.

— 5 —

Think positive

What thoughts went through your mind as you read the title of this chapter? Perhaps 'How am I supposed to think positively when I haven't a job or even the prospect of getting one?' Or maybe 'Being told to think positive is rather like being told to "snap out of it"; doesn't she think I would if only I could?' Or even 'It's all very well for *her*. How can she understand the way I feel?'

I will answer these questions in reverse order:

1 I can understand how you feel because I've been there. I too have been out of work when I would far rather have had a job to go to. So I *do* understand your feelings because they have been my feelings too.

2 Being told to 'snap out of it' when you are feeling depressed makes it seem as though there is a special switch which, when flicked, will automatically dispel all your cares – and we all know this just isn't so. Positive thinking, on the other hand, is a slower and more deliberate process which is not designed necessarily to change the situation around you, but to help you to cope while in the midst of it.

3 While accepting that it may be difficult to become a positive thinker when you are without a job, it is certainly not impossible – and I can assure you that, if you do not try to do so, you are far less likely to be considered for a job in the future. Don't become one of those people who believes that it is only possible to be positive when everything in life is going wonderfully – you might have a very long wait! After all, how many people do you know whose life is so perfect that they have nothing at all to worrry about? The clever person is the one who learns to think as positively as possible during the hard times, not just when everything is plain sailing.

Someone who has a talent for living – whatever life may throw at them – realises that today is all you can be sure of. Whatever happened in the past, it has gone and nothing in the world can alter it. However much we might try to plan and prepare for the future, there are too many imponderables for us to be absolutely certain how it is going to turn out. The only thing you have is *now*. So, even if the now does not offer you everything you would like, take the time and trouble to look for, notice and relish the good things it does offer you.

There is a well-known epitaph (although whether it is real or invented I do not know) which states: 'Here lies someone who was going to be happy tomorrow'. Too many people are relying upon some future event to give them the happiness they seek. You must have met many of them. 'I'll be so happy when I leave school', they say. Or 'When I have a better job . . . When I get married . . . When I have a baby . . . When we own our own home . . . When the children go off to college . . . When I have grandchildren . . . When I'm rich . . .' But what are they going to do with all the intervening years – just sit and wait for them to pass? What a waste of life!

Instead of becoming one of those 'I'll be happy when . . .' people, why not try finding something to be positive about right now? You will find it brings many bonuses.

• You will be far nicer to have around. We have already seen how important other people are when things are not going too well. But other people are not going to want to spend much time in your company if you always concentrate on the negative aspects of life.

- By demonstrating a positive attitude you are far more likely to attract positive happenings. It does not matter whether you believe that this is because of some natural law whereby positivity attracts positivity, or simply that someone who is being as optimistic and confident as possible will be more likely to notice and take advantage of any opportunities which may present themselves.

- You will get more enjoyment out of life – and, since, this may be the only one you have, that seems to me to be a pretty important bonus.

Living in the present moment also helps to dispel fear from the mind. Most fear is really anxiety over something which *might* happen some time in the future and, since we are only capable of thinking one thought at a time, if you are concentrating on the good things which exist at present you cannot be worrying about all those things which might go wrong tomorrow.

Fear also has a paralysing effect so that you become less active and less able to do something to improve your present circumstances. If you are to make changes in yourself and your life, you need to be as active as possible rather than allowing yourself to be tethered to the spot by fear.

Positive thinking, of course, will not work if you are simply paying lip-service to it. You must really believe all those optimistic thoughts and phrases. There is no point in pronouncing the words 'I know that things are going to get better', if there is a little voice deep within you saying 'I don't really think they will but I suppose I ought to keep repeating it'.

If you believe in yourself, other people are far more likely to do the same. This becomes particularly important should the time come when you find yourself in an interview situation. Put yourself in the interviewer's position. Suppose you have two applicants between whom there is little to choose on paper. They come from similar backgrounds, and have the same qualifications and years of experience. There they sit in front of you, one looking at you confidently exuding positivity while the other is staring at the ground obviously waiting to be rejected. Which is the one you would pick as being most likely to be an asset to your company?

Even if you have not reached the stage of an interview – or if there is some reason why that is not likely to happen – carrying an aura of positivity will stand you in good stead in other circumstances. If you decide to go for retraining, you will be able to get far more from whatever course you are taking if you believe in your ability to absorb skills and knowledge. If you choose to join a social group of some kind, you will find it easier to become accepted by others if you appear to be eager to take part and to give as well as receive. You may be a wonderful person with a heart of gold – but that is very difficult to spot if you spend much of your time sitting quietly by yourself in a corner.

Remember that the attitude you display is the one you will find mirrored back to you by those with whom you come into contact. If you present a despondent, world-weary face to others, it will not take very long before they begin to reflect the same attitude. This, in turn, will make you feel even more depressed so that, before long, everyone will be extremely negative and thoroughly miserable.

You owe it to those around you to be as positive as possible without being dishonest. There is nothing wrong with telling those closest to you that you are disappointed with the situation as it now is, *provided* you then go on to tell them what you intend to do about it. You will find that friends and family will soon rally round you, and will go out of their way to seek your company – and this will certainly help to rebuild a fractured self-esteem.

There is no point listing all your woes to more casual acquaintances – although there is no harm in calmly letting them know what the situation is. This not only saves possible embarrassment in the future, but you never know who will just happen to hear of a job which might be appropriate for you.

Here again, it is far more important to emphasise the fact that you intend to do something to ameliorate the situation so that you give the impression of being just the kind of person any discerning employer would be seeking.

Positivity case histories

Let's have a look at two different case histories and see how the people concerned were able to develop their positivity, and how this helped them become more fulfilled and get more enjoyment out of life.

JOHN

By the time he retired at 65, John had spent almost 40 years working in the motor industry. Starting on the factory floor, he had worked his way up to supervisor and had then been asked to represent his team on the board. He had loved every minute of it – from his apprenticeship to the chance to mix with members of the management team and have some influence on the way things were done.

John had always been a workaholic. In busy times, if extra hands were needed to do overtime or to work at weekends, John was the first to volunteer. When the board of management wanted someone to visit other companies to compare working methods, John was there. He told himself that he loved his wife and children – and he probably did in his own way – but he was a preoccupied husband and frequently an absent father.

As his 65th birthday approached, John tried to put all thoughts of retirement out of his mind. After all, he was on the board now. But the company's policy of compulsory retirement at that age applied to management just as to the work force and suddenly the day arrived. There was a party with a speech and a presentation and, when it was over, John had no option but to leave.

He woke up next morning to find that his life had changed beyond recognition. Suddenly he seemed to have nowhere to go and nothing to do. He began to ask himself whether he had any purpose at all in life. He looked at his wife, busy with her various committees, her friends and her classes, and marvelled at the way she had learned to fill her day. Nothing appeared to lie in front of him except long, boring hours of inactivity.

At this point John had to try and find some way of filling the day. Several times he wandered down into town hoping to bump into one of his friends with whom he could have a cup of coffee and a talk. This did not happen very often but, on the occasions when it did, all John could talk about was how much he had enjoyed his job, how he missed it and how he felt that there was little now to look forward to. Small wonder that his friends began to go out of their way to avoid meeting him. Becoming gradually aware of this, John told himself that, now he was no longer working, he had become a boring person with nothing to talk about. This was partly true, but the principal reason was that he had never bothered to develop an interest in anything other than work. He did not even take the trouble to ask those he met about *their* families, *their* lives or *their* interests. He was so busy wallowing in his own negativity that he was oblivious to how anyone else was feeling.

By the time I met him, John had been retired for nearly a year – and his personal situation had grown worse. He had reached the stage where he would lie in bed for hours in the morning so that the day itself would be shorter. He had cut himself off from his former friends and even found it difficult to communicate with his wife, so resentful was he of her wide circle of acquaintances and variety of interests. He was under so much stress that he had begun to suffer from a series of aches and pains for which the doctor could find no physical cause.

There was little point at this stage in telling John that he should have started preparing for his retirement long before the day arrived. But, of course, that is just what he should have done. Had he begun to develop hobbies, interests or group activities in the years before his 65th birthday, he would have found himself looking forward with pleasure to his retirement when he would have more time to devote to those pursuits.

We started by trying to take stock of the current position. I asked John what was good about being retired and in what ways he considered himself fortunate. At first I had to cut him short as he began to tell me of all the things he regretted. Finally he came up with the following:

● he no longer had to get up early on cold winter mornings;

● no more traffic jams;

● he and wife were both healthy;

● with his pension and their savings, they had sufficient money to live relatively well;

● they would no longer have to take their annual holiday at the height of the season when the plant closed;

● their two children were happily married with children of their own . . .

And there he stopped; he could not think of anything else.

I asked him whether he had any ideas about how he would like to spend his time in the future. Apart from telling me that he really wanted to get to know his grandchildren in a way that he had never had time to know his own children, there seemed to be nothing. He really had no hobbies or interest in anything except cars and engines, and there seemed little opportunity to indulge these.

Could he perhaps think of a way in which that interest could be combined with getting to know his grandchildren? Somewhat hesitantly he ventured that he might take the two older children to the veteran car rally to be held the following week. He began to warm to the idea, suggesting that he might take them out to lunch first at a popular local hamburger bar. His eyes brightened and he started to speak more quickly as ideas came to him.

Suddenly John had something to look forward to, something to tell his wife about when he saw her that evening and something to get up for in the morning. It was only a small beginning, but I knew that, once he developed a taste for positivity, it would increase.

I did not see John for some time after that, but several months later I had a letter from him telling me that he now saw his grandchildren regularly, he and his wife had decided to take up golf, and he was teaching car maintenance at a local adult education centre. Life was worth living again. In fact he did not know how he had ever found time to go to work!

CAROLINE

Caroline had been a senior secretary in an insurance company for ten years and, even though she knew there were redundancies in the offing, she had considered her job to be safe. Unfortunately, however, the man she worked for had been made redundant and so she too had to go.

Initially Caroline thought that she would find another position quite quickly, but this proved not to be the case. She wasn't offered any interviews; in fact most organisations did not even bother to reply to her letters of application. Soon she began to look at all those job advertisements with such a jaundiced eye – 'This one wants someone under thirty' . . . 'I don't stand a chance of getting that one' . . . 'This one would mean too much travelling' . . . 'There are bound to be hundreds of applicants for that one'.

The days dragged on and Caroline sat at home, growing ever more despondent, her redundancy pay dwindling rapidly. What was she going to go? Suppose she never was able to find another job. She was on the scrap heap at 36. Thinking that her friends must be looking down on her and considering her a failure, she began to cut herself off from them, refusing all invitations and responding curtly when they telephoned. When they stopped calling, she was able to tell herself that she had been right all along and that her 'friends' didn't want to know a failure.

Eventually she became so depressed that she consulted her doctor who put her on a short course of anti-depressant tablets. These, of course, did nothing to alleviate the situation, but succeeded in making Caroline so lethargic that she did not even feel like tidying her flat or doing her shopping; on some days she did not even bother to get dressed but spent all day lounging around in her dressing gown. Fortunately she realised what was happening to her and that she needed help – and this is how I came to meet her.

Unlike John, Caroline knew precisely what she wanted for the future – another job. But how was she to get one when she could not even persuade anyone to interview her? I asked her to consider what was positive in her life at present, as well as what her particular skills or capabilities were. This was her list:

- she knew that she was a good secretary – fast and efficient with considerable organisational skills;

- being unmarried and with no children, she had no one else depending upon her;

- her redundancy pay was sufficient to pay the mortgage on her flat and her day-to-day expenses for some time.

I asked Caroline about her hopes for the future and she told me she would love to be able to work for herself so that no one could ever make her redundant again; nor would she ever have to go through what she felt was the humiliating process of job-hunting.

Was there any way in which she could combine her skills and her desires? Only by setting up as a freelance secretary, she supposed. I asked her what this would entail and she told me that some hotels and conference centres regularly employed free-lance secretarial staff. Would she enjoy doing such work? Oh, yes – but they probably had all the contacts they needed.

I asked her whether she would consider having some business cards printed and approaching the various centres. She hesitated. What would be the worst scenario if she did so? She feared that no one would want her. Apart from the cost of printing the cards and wasting some of her time (of which she had plenty at the moment), would she actually be any worse off if they all turned her down? She admitted that she would not.

'So if that is the worst that can happen, anything else must be better?'

'Yes.'

'Surely it is worth trying?'

'I suppose it is,' she agreed.

Caroline was not a person to do things by halves. She did not stop at distributing her business cards in appropriate places. She joined the Enterprise Allowance Scheme which gave her a regular – if small – income, and used this to take out advertisements and write to organisations, offering to do secretarial work for them on a freelance basis. She also attended all the free business seminars to which she was entitled, so that she was able to develop a marketing strategy and deal effectively with the financial aspects of her new business.

The business itself started slowly, but Caroline's reputation for efficiency and reliability soon grew – and so did her confidence and her belief in herself.

Logic and emotion

You will see from the way in which the two people above dealt with their problems that, in order to think positively, it is necessary to use a combination of logic and emotion. Our instinctive reaction to crises is emotional; sometimes the degree of emotion is such that it seems to paralyse the logical part of the brain so that we 'feel' more and more, and seem able to 'think' less and less.

There is nothing wrong with allowing yourself the indulgence of emotion as the initial response to a situation, but the sooner you can bring in the logical aspect the sooner you will be able to do something to make changes happen.

If you find yourself faced with a crisis situation, try following these steps.

1 Acknowledge your emotional response. Analyse how you feel. Are you hurt, bitter, angry, frightened . . .?

2 Once that initial reaction has been acknowledged, ask yourself whether it was justified. If everyone else in the world has been offered a job then perhaps the rejection *is* personal. But if it is an unfortunate sign of the times that millions are unable to find work, then, unhappy as you may be about the situation, you know that you have not been singled out as being particularly unworthy.

3 In what way are you fortunate? Do you have a loving family, a pleasant home? Have you particular skills or interests? The very fact that you have eyes with which to read these words and a brain with which to understand them makes you luckier than some.

4 What do you want to happen in the future? Is it possible? You must have a direction in which to aim; even if you do not reach that particular target, going some way towards it will give you the positivity and optimism to make the best of the point you do reach. And you may find you go further than you ever dreamed would be possible.

5 Take some time to work out how you can combine your aims and your capabilities to achieve your desired end. Take the first step *now* – even if that first step consists only

of obtaining information. You will feel far more positive once you have done something.

Visualisation

Visualisation, which we looked at briefly in Chapter 3, is an essential part of being positive. It enables you to do more than pay lip-service to what you want to achieve; it helps you to 'see' it as though you had already done so.

Too little credit is given to the power of visualisation. And yet many people have been using it in a negative way for a long time. Every time you tell yourself that you are bound to fail and imagine yourself doing so, you are in fact programming yourself for failure. If I were to lay a 6-inch wide plank of wood on the ground and ask you to walk along it, you probably would not have any trouble doing so. If I were to fix that same piece of wood between the roofs of two buildings and ask you to walk along it, you would probably refuse. Why? It is the same piece of wood and you have the same size feet. But, as soon as I mention that the plank may be about 30 feet from the ground, what happens? You begin to imagine what would happen should you fall – you visualise the situation and, having done so, you prob-ably *would* fall if you attempt the exercise.

If negative visualisation is so effective, it follows that positive visualisation works too. You only have to listen to some of the world's most famous athletes to realise that, in addition to developing great skill in their chosen sport, they have also learned to visualise themselves giving wonderful performances. It is a technique I use all the time when treating those who suffer from phobias – and I promise you that it works.

So, once you have decided what it is that you want, set aside 15 or 20 minutes *every day* for your visualisation. The very act of harnessing the power of your imagination in this way will make an imprint on your subconscious mind and cause you to feel more positive.

The stages of a visualisation technique are as follows.

1 Sit or lie comfortably and take the time to relax each set of muscles in turn.

2 Close your eyes, and breathe slowly and evenly, listening to the rhythm of your breathing.

3 Now imagine the end result for which you are aiming as if it had already happened. Don't try and work out how you achieved it and don't just work on the first step you need to take. What you need to see in your imagination is just how things would look if success were already yours.

4 Although this is primarily a visual technique, try and incorporate feelings too. How would you *feel* if the scene you are picturing was already reality?

5 If negative thoughts should intrude, don't increase your tension by trying to *force* them out. Either place them to one side in your mind or allow them into the image and deal with them as you would in reality.

For example, when I started working with Caroline on her visualisation she was still finding it difficult to imagine that things could ever go right for her. In her mental image she had already set up her office with a desk and computer/word processor. One day she told me that, every time she tried to visualise the scene, something went wrong with her word processor when she had urgent work to do and, as she could not get rid of that thought, she felt unable to continue. I asked her what she would do if a word processor she was using really did go wrong in such circumstances. She thought for a while and then said that she had at least two friends who owned similar machines, and she knew that, in an emergency, she would be able to borrow one of these. I suggested that she should deal with the imagined crisis in precisely that way and continue with her visualisation – which she was then able to do.

Positive and negative talk

If you are to become more positive, you must pay attention to the way you talk to yourself and the way you talk *about* yourself.

Negative self-talk induces negative visualisation, so be on the look-out for such phrases as 'I was stupid to . . .' 'If only I were (younger, cleverer etc.) . . .', 'They won't want someone like me'.

Every time you say something negative about yourself, you reinforce your inner belief, so stop apologising for yourself. 'I've always been shy', 'I'm not very good at . . .'. Not only will such phrases convince the person you are speaking to (after all, why should they think you would lie to them?), they will convince *you* too. Why not try acting and speaking in an enthusiastic way, and allow your positivity to convince your subconscious mind that this is the type of person you really are?

You will have heard the old joke about 'Which do you want first, the good news or the bad news?' When speaking about yourself to other people, make sure you give the good news first. This is not the same as being over-vain or blowing your own trumpet; it is a way of giving positive information about yourself, your interests and your enthusiasms.

Body language

Remember that you do not communicate only with words; your body language says a great deal about you and how you are feeling, so make sure that yours is positive:

- look people in the eye as you speak to them;

- try to stand in a way that is upright but not rigid – hunched shoulders always look negative;

- relax your hands and arms and avoid fidgeting, never fold your arms across your chest;

- avoid such habits as lip-biting or fiddling with coins in your pocket;

- smile naturally when appropriate.

—————— *Be kind to yourself* ——————

It is very hard to be positive if you don't like and appreciate yourself. So, in addition to the exercise you have already prac- tised of thinking about yourself as a terrific person, go out of your way to pamper yourself to give yourself little treats from time to time. These do not have to cost money and will depend on how you like to enjoy yourself – perhaps a long, leisurely bath, a walk with the dog or just sitting listening quietly to music. By going out of your way to create these pleasant interludes, for no other reason than that you enjoy them, you will be informing your subconscious that you consider yourself a special person, worthy of such treats.

As you take each step on the road to your desired goal, stop and give yourself credit for what you have achieved. However great or small the amount of progress, you have made a positive move towards a better future and that is something to be proud of.

If you make mistakes – and we all do – see them for what they are, a learning process. Instead of castigating yourself for being a fool or wasting time, pause and analyse whether what you did was so wrong, what you have learned from it and what you would do differently next time.

Don't give up

The difference between the positive and negative thinker is that the former will be able to think creatively about whatever disappointments or setbacks are encountered. Look at such situations as possibilities for change and improvement. As Vera Peiffer says in her book *Strategies of Optimism* (Element), 'Life is not about guarantees; it is about opportunities'.

Avoid programming your mind negatively by using the words 'always' or 'never' too often. Repeat 'I always make a mess of . . .' or 'I will never be able to . . .' often enough and you will come to believe it. So will the people to whom you say those words, so you will automatically reduce your chances of being considered a competent and effective person.

Review your day

Allow yourself about ten minutes at the end of your day to reflect on what you have been doing. But make sure that those reflections are positive ones. Ask yourself what has gone well for you and what you have achieved – and these achievements can be quite small ones. Perhaps you managed to cope with the children without losing your temper; you may have written a long over-due letter; or perhaps you completed the day's tasks more quickly and efficiently than usual. When was the last time you gave yourself credit for such things? We are all so good at thinking 'If only I hadn't said that' or 'I should have done this'.

When you find, as you will, that ending your day with positive thoughts makes you feel better in yourself, you might like to extend the process so that you help others feel better too. Don't just criticise them when they have done something which displeases you; mention any positive words, attitudes or actions on their part. The knowledge that you have made someone else feel good will create a good sensation in you too.

Change your inner script

It is very difficult to break the habit of negative thinking, so try to become aware of when your thoughts are damaging your self-image. If you make a mistake or something does not turn out as you wished, rather than saying to yourself 'I am an idiot, why do I always get it wrong?', try thinking 'Now I got something wrong there. If I were to do it again, how would I do it differently?'

If you find yourself thinking self-critical thoughts, ask yourself what it would be more useful to think. When you catch yourself anticipating something with dread or defeatism, stop and create a positive visualisation for yourself so that your mind accepts the likelihood of a successful outcome.

What do you believe?

Whatever your beliefs about the meaning and purpose of life – or indeed whether or not you have any – can influence the degree of positivity or negativity you feel.

Suppose you believe that this life is all there is and that once you are dead, that is it. If that is the case, then each step we take along the way must be of tremendous importance – after all, this is not a dress rehearsal, it is the real thing. So don't waste time regretting what has gone or concentrating on a present situation over which you have no control – ask yourself what you can do to make some improvement in the present and to create a future to look forward to. Hold on to your dream, not what someone else thinks would be best for you so that, whether you have 5 days left or 50 years, they can be as positive, purposeful and fulfilling as possible.

Perhaps, however, you believe that this life is just part of a much greater pattern – even if you are not quite sure what that pattern is and how you fit into it. If that is the case, life must contain a series of lessons to be learnt, so that we develop and evolve along the way. Some people like to think of these learning opportunities as tests to prove we are worthy of whatever we think comes to us when this present life is over. I prefer to call them opportunities, giving us the chance to grow both practically and spiritually.

If your beliefs incorporate the concept of reincarnation, then what you learn and achieve in this life will affect the problems, opportunities and evolvement of the next and future ones. Should you give up when faced with a certain set of problems in this lifetime, you will probably find yourself faced with them again next time.

I am not trying to inflict any particular set of beliefs upon you or to convert you to any specific way of thinking. All I would point out is that, whatever your feelings, the here and now, and how you deal with it, is of great significance.

— 6 —

Discover those hidden talents

If you find yourself without a job, the one thing you probably have in abundance is time. Whether you look on that fact as a tragedy or a blessing depends upon you and your outlook.

Some people in your position would consider having all this time on their hands as a heavy burden. What can they possibly do to fill the hours between waking in the morning and going to bed at night? But that is a very negative outlook and you have just discovered the benefits of being positive, haven't you? So try looking on all this free time as a bonus, a gift which may provide you with an opportunity to learn more about yourself, develop existing interests and cultivate new ones.

Whether you are young or old, fit or housebound, there are any number of different possibilities for you to pursue. I have known many people who have found great pleasure in ways which may well have surprised their friends – from the 42-year-old man who had always wanted to learn to tap dance to the woman in her 70s who, having gone into service at the age of 14, decided to indulge herself by enjoying some of the education she had never been allowed to have. The year she became a great-grandmother she also acquired two GCSEs (in English and history).

Discover those hidden talents

Finding a new hobby, interest or outlet for your enthusiasm does more than simply pass the time. It can give you a whole new lease of life, providing more for you to talk about and therefore making you a more interesting person to be with. It can be a way of making new friends and acquaintances because you do not have to follow these pursuits alone. Learning something new is always stimulating and you may even discover that you have a talent you never knew existed.

Developing an enthusiastic approach to whatever you decide to embark on even helps your mental and physical health. When we are excited about something, we breathe more deeply. This increases the flow of oxygen to the brain and we feel our spirits being lifted. This surge of oxygen also improves circulation and encourages the release of toxins from the body. And, of course, the better you feel, the more you are likely to be able to under-take. Thus, your interests might spread, your day become even fuller and your circle of friends grow wider.

So you have accepted the concept of developing your interests – but where should you start? How are you to know which would be the best direction for you? You may feel, particularly if finances are restricted, that you cannot afford costly mistakes. (Although it must be said that none of the ideas given here need cost very much at all; of course the budding artist could go out and purchase the very best set of oil paints, complete with wooden carrying case and sable brushes. But it is also possible to achieve stunning results with a simple water-colour set – or even a stick of charcoal.)

To determine the best direction for you to follow – or at any rate the first one – try asking yourself the following questions.

- *What do I know I enjoy?*   Have you been an avid reader since childhood? Then perhaps you might like to try your hand at writing. If you are always attracted by art exhibitions and galleries, you might choose to learn some form of painting or drawing. Ardent followers of light opera could perhaps join a local amateur company. Even if initially their contribution was mostly backstage, they would still have the thrill of being involved in the performance.

—— 81 ——

- *What have I done in the past?* You already have a head start if you know that you used to love making collages or working with wood. Quite often such interests have to take second (or third or even tenth) place when you are studying, working or bringing up a family. Perhaps this is the time when you can rekindle old interests and develop them to a greater degree.

- *Have I any secret ambitions?* Like George who had always wanted to learn to tap dance, but whose father considered such pursuits 'unmanly', there may be some secret yearning within you which you can now fulfil. And don't be afraid of being the odd one out at a particular class or group meeting. George was the only man in his tap class and the only person over 30 but, not only did he thoroughly enjoy the lessons, he found he was being thoroughly spoilt by his co-students. If there is any area of your life where you can say 'I wish I had . . .', now is your chance to go ahead and do it.

- *Do I already have any particular skills?* If you stop and think about yourself, your abilities and your aptitudes, you will probably find yourself being pointed in a particular direction. Do you have the kind of enquiring mind which would be fascinated by the research needed for a specific piece of writing? Have you always been told that you have a real flair for colour and design? Perhaps you have the kind of patience and love of detail which would allow you to enjoy intricate and long-term projects of a fine nature. Don't sell yourself short at this point; it is easy to believe that yours is a very little talent and that everyone else's must be far more developed. But we are not talking here about making a career out of your creativity (although that may well follow), but about pursuing an interest which gives you pleasure. I used to attend a portrait painting class, working in oils. Although the sitters were just about recognisable from the portraits I painted, neither I nor most of the others in the class were great artists and I don't suppose anyone would have wanted to buy our work. But we had a wonderful time increasing our skills and developing a great sense of camaraderie – and my later efforts were certainly far better than the earlier ones.

- *What are my limitations?* If you have never been able to stick a handle on a cup without breaking one or the other, if you like to tackle jobs which show immediate results or if you are tone deaf, you will already have some indication of which pursuits are *not* for you. There could be other limitations too. You might be confined to home because of existing commitments and responsibilities, or you might have some disability which prevents you performing certain actions with ease. Money might be very tight – but, you will see, when we come to look at individual possibilities, that this does not necesarily matter.

By the time you have asked and answered all those questions, you should have some idea of the path you wish to follow. But perhaps you would rather try something completely new – only you don't yet know what that is. A good source of information is usually your nearest public library. Most have leaflet tables and noticeboards giving details of local clubs and organisations, and you may glean inspiration from these.

Another idea is to contact your nearest adult education centre to find out what courses and classes they offer. These are usually quite inexpensive for those without a wage and there is the advantage that you can often use their equipment rather than having to pay for your own. And, should you be taking up potentially costly subjects such as computer graphics, photography, weaving or pottery, this can be a very considerable benefit.

It is not possible in a single chapter to cover every possible outlet for your creativity, but here are some examples and the various ways in which you can pursue them. Even if none of the ideas given appeal particularly to you, you can use them as a basis for further thought.

Music

There are so many ways in which you can enjoy music. You can be as active or as passive as you wish.

Perhaps all you want to do is sit quietly in a chair in your own home, listening to whatever is your favourite type of music. If that is the case, you don't even have to go to the expense of purchasing all those records, cassettes or compact discs. Most libraries now have a music section from which it is possible to borrow anything from Chris Barber to concertos, from *Peer Gynt* to *Phantom of the Opera*.

If listening in comfort is your choice, you do not have to do this alone. There may be many others who would enjoy the opportunity to share good music and good company, and musical evenings are not difficult to arrange. You would be indulging in a pastime which interests you, while extending your social circle at the same time.

Of course, you may prefer to indulge your musical interest more actively. Making music can take many forms, from joining a local folk club to a singsong round the piano in someone's front room. You could learn (or relearn) to play a musical instrument – it's funny how practising no longer seems a chore when you are *choosing* to do it rather than being forced to.

If you are already proficient at playing a particular instrument, how would you feel about teaching others? You could do it purely for your own and your pupil's enjoyment or you might even find it an extra source of income. If you don't feel you wish to work with often unwilling children, you could offer to teach adults only. There are many who never had the chance to learn to play an instrument as a child who would love to do so now –

not to reach concert standard but for their own enjoyment. If you are interested in helping those less fortunate than yourself, here too you will find opportunities. You might provide entertainment for those in old people's homes or hospitals – and you could either do this alone or join together with other musicians to provide an entire programme. Many people with severe learning difficulties have been found to respond well to music, but there are so few people with the time and inclination to share it with them. Could you consider offering to help?

Perhaps you could go one stage further and try your hand at composing. You do not have to attempt symphonies or grand opera if these are not your area of interest. But you may find that a local school or organisation would love someone to write the score for their forthcoming Christmas pantomime. Or you could simply compose for your own pleaure, either creating something entirely new or setting one of your favourite poems to music.

Writing

Many people have an inner desire to write but, because it can be such a time-consuming exercise, it is difficult to fit it in when you have a full-time job or are bringing up a family. But now is your chance. Now you have the time to start that novel you have always wanted to write or compose poetry – whether for pleasure or profit.

Even if you begin to write simply for your own enjoyment, it can be a means of earning a little extra money. You are unlikely – unless you have a particular talent and are prepared to devote a great deal of time to it – to make a fortune. However, local magazines are often looking for articles from people living in the area and even contributions to the letters' page of women's magazines can earn anything from £5 to £20.

If you have not written anything since your school essays, you could begin by either attending a creative writing class at your local adult education centre or joining one of the writers' groups which can be found in most towns. The class would give you the opportunity to learn the basics of your craft, while the writers' group would allow you to read or listen to the work of others while offering your own efforts for constructive criticism.

This is not nearly as daunting as it sounds. There is a widely-held but mistaken belief that all local writers' groups consist of published authors. In fact there is, in most cases, a wide cross-section of people. In my experience you will find a few published authors (ranging from members who have had published a couple of verses, through the article writers to those who have written one or more books). I have always found such group members completely lacking in ego and extremely generous with their advice, so they are a tremendous asset at any meeting.

Some members of writers' groups have no desire whatsoever to see their work published. They write just for the pleasure it brings them and the group meetings are their forum. Because such people probably spend more time revising and perfecting each word or phrase than those who are attempting to write for publication, their efforts are usually delightful and there is much to be learned from them. Of course, it is possible that, even if you begin by wanting to write for your own pleasure, you may one day – often with the encouragement of your group – decide to submit some of your efforts for possible publication. The choice is yours.

Don't feel that, if you are a very new writer, you would not be welcome at a writers' group. Much of the success of their meetings depends upon having a wide range of talents and interests present, and I have always found the praise and encouragement to be generous, and the criticism kind and constructive. And, as someone who has belonged to such a group for some years, there is a particular and genuine joy to be experienced by each person when one of the newer members has their first piece published.

Of course you may not be interested in sharing your writing in a group situation; you may just want to sit at home and write for your own pleasure – or there may be some reason why you are unable to attend meetings on a regular basis. It still does not have to be a lonely pastime. You could join a manuscript circle whereby each member submits a piece of writing and the contributions are circulated together in a single envelope from one member to another so that each can read them all and make comments if they wish.

Arthur retired from his job in a security firm just before his 67th birthday. Because his work was quite routine, he had enjoyed writing as a hobby over the years. Not considering himself a creative person, he had written mostly articles and factual pieces, a few of which had been published in some of the more specialist magazines. He decided to continue writing after his retirement. He turned the spare bedroom into a small office and decided that he would write in the mornings only, leaving the afternoons free to spend with his wife doing all those things they had looked forward to for so long.

Over the next year or so Arthur continued to write his articles – only now he had more time to devote to making contact with individual editors, and becoming known to them as someone who was both meticulous and reliable. By the time he reached his 70th birthday his articles were appearing in various magazines with consistent regularity. In fact, as he told me, he was now earning nearly as much during his retirement as he had when he had worked full-time for the security company.

One of the most pleasurable forms of writing is creating a book of memories for your children, grandchildren and even great-grandchildren. Life changes so rapidly now that the things you remember from your childhood (even if you are no more than 30 years old) may seem novel and fascinating to the next generation. When my sons (born in the early 1960s) were small children there were no personal computers, videos or camcorders and few homes as yet had freezers or microwave cookers. When I was a child we did not have central heating, television or automatic washing machines; there were steam trains, sweet rationing, coal merchants – and the milkman had a horse. My own mother talks of taking the rice pudding to the baker to be cooked slowly in the cooling bread oven while my father told me how he made his own wireless set and, when the time came for him to buy his first car, he was simply shown how the controls worked and then allowed to take it away – no driving tests then. Think how fascinating this sort of information can be to a child and how tragic it would be if all these memories died with the people of a particular generation. For they may not be the stuff of which history books are made – but they probably provide a truer picture of a specific era than any academic tome. I can still remember the amazement on one small boy's face when the television programme *Blue Peter* showed the rations allowed to each person during the Second World War. Having (in common with many small boys) a healthy appetite, he simply did not believe that anyone could have survived on the rations shown.

If only everyone could be encouraged to compile a record of early memories, what a source of knowledge this could be for future generations. And it is the small and seemingly trivial things which are the most fascinating, as you will see if you look at a copy of an old newspaper printed before you were born. If you really feel that it would be beyond you to write anything of this sort, you could try recording it on a number of cassettes. It does not take long to forget about the microphone and all you have to do is speak your memories as if telling them to an interested child.

Art

What a wide area the word 'art' covers! You might feel that you would simply like to know more about painting, drawing and their history, or you may wish to be more practical and learn to develop or improve your own skills.

For someone who has the time, there is a whole world of art to be discovered – and there are many different ways of doing this so you are bound to find one which suits you.

Going to great lengths to see for yourself the great works of genius is a wonderful experience, but it can prove costly in both time and money. But there are some excellent books available which you should be able to borrow from your local library at no cost at all. You might find that in your area there is either a club or a class dedicated to art appreciation, where you would not only be able to look at some of the more famous works, but also learn something about the artist and his or her background. This would give you the opportunity to meet others with a similar interest and to discuss the topic – and perhaps go out together to visit art exhibitions.

Many towns and certainly all British cities, have a local museum and art gallery – and in most areas these are either very inexpensive to enter or they are completely free. You may not be interested in every exhibit you see but the range is usually so wide that you are sure to find something you can appreciate. And keep an eye open for local art exhibitions in your own or the surrounding area; some of the work shown at these exhibitions is of a very high standard indeed.

However much you enjoy looking at work created by other people, if you were to try your hand at drawing or painting I think you would soon find that doing can be far more rewarding than viewing. Don't worry if you think you cannot draw a straight line when you want to or if you have never held a paintbrush in your life. No one is asking you to create works which are worthy of being sold – or even of being hung on the wall. This does not mean, however, that you might not discover a latent talent within you which only needs to be developed for you to achieve a very high standard.

Everyone has to begin somewhere. You could join a class – there are usually several in each district. And you have one advantage over those people in work. In every area in which I have lived, the evening art classes are the first ones to be filled and many applicants are disappointed. But there is usually a greater availability of places during the day, so you should be able to find one to suit you.

What medium you choose to employ is up to you, but may be governed by cost as well as by preference. Oil painting is very satisfying (and has the advantage that you can easily paint over your mistakes without them showing through), but it can be expensive – and the pictures can be more awkward to carry around. However, if you are attending a class where the easels, palettes etc. are provided, remember that you need only about eight tubes of paint and three or four good brushes to start with. Water-colours are smaller, lighter and less expensive, but you may not find them satisfying enough if you are someone who enjoys great, bold splashes of colour.

Charcoal is cheap, the effects can be achieved quite quickly and can be pleasingly dramatic – and, with the assistance of a putty rubber, you can learn to add highlights which give depth and form to your work. Coloured pastels are pleasing – if messy – and are usually contained in a single box. When rubbed with cloth or finger they can be blended to provide a paint-like coverage and texture.

Of course you may not want to join others at all, but prefer to sit in your garden working on your own. This is fine if you have painted or drawn before but, if you are a beginner you may soon find yourself becoming disheartened without other people to encourage and support you. Sharing the experience with one or more other people does also make it easier if you decide to go out into the countryside to paint when it might be unwise for a lone artist to do so.

Don't worry about whether you are 'any good' or not. After all, appreciation of art is purely subjective. You and I could stand and look at the same painting, and one of us might love it and the other hate it. Who is to say who is right and who is wrong? And if you watch a really talented artist at work, you will see that even he or she will often begin by daubing what look like random blocks of colour on the paper or canvas. No one's opening strokes are going to provide a satisfying image so don't allow yourself to be put off by well-meaning friends who lean over your shoulder and ask you 'What's that funny green bit meant to be?'

The story is told that soon after Winston Churchill began to paint – which he did quite late in life – he was sitting at his easel on the estate of a titled friend, staring at a blank canvas and not knowing quite how to begin. He decided that the sky was blue and he dipped his brush tentatively into the blue paint and applied a tiny daub of it at the top left-hand corner of the canvas. He had not gone much further when the owner of the land came along. Taking the brush from Churchill's hand she drew a line from side to side, about half-way down the canvas. The upper half she covered in a mid-blue wash and the lower half in a mid-green. 'Now,' she said to Churchill, 'build on that'. And of course she had the right idea; be brave, get rid of the white and make a start. Whether your finished effort is brilliant or not is nothing when compared with how much you are able to enjoy yourself.

Many years ago a friend and I were painting at the edge of Epping Forest. Now, in my heart I am an Impressionist with a great desire to paint the wind in the trees and the light on the water. Unfortunately my brain and my hand did not know this at that time, and so my work was far too detailed; you could see every leaf on every tree and every blade of grass on the ground. When I turned to look at my friend's efforts, she had done just what I wanted to do – her picture was not made up of details, but of the effects of light and shade. I complimented her on her achievement, but she told me that it had not been deliberate – she had simply forgotten her spectacles and was not able to see any of the finer details in the first place!

Even those who are housebound or disabled can enjoy painting and drawing. You can work from your imagination, or from photographs or postcards. If you are unable to get out, you could ask one or more friends to come and join you for a regular session. One of the main reasons for involving other people is that it will *make* you do something on a regular basis, whereas we all know how easy it is to put things off when you are on your own.

Crafts

There are almost as many forms of handicraft as there are people wishing to practise them. Some are delicate and dainty – tapestry, lace making, pressed flower work – while others are heavy and robust – wood-turning, basket making, wrought-iron work. But all of them can be satisfying – and often profitable. You might either be able to sell what you create or save yourself money by giving the results of your work as birthday and Christmas presents.

The craft you choose will depend on many things. Obviously personal preference plays a large part: there is no point in spending time and effort creating something you do not really like when it is finished. But your choice will also be governed by such things as the space you have available, your finances, and your own strength and fitness.

Here are some examples of people who have turned their love and interest of a particular craft to profitable use:

● A retired widower who began making articles in wrought-iron for his own home. His work is of such high standard that friends soon began asking him to make things for them too. Before long he was producing items to be sold in local shops, and at craft fairs up and down the country.

● A young mother with three small children who made herself a flower press from two pieces of wood and some blotting paper. The cards and pictures she created from the petals she dried (taken from flowers in her own garden) soon became well known in the district and she was asked to run an evening course at the local adult education centre.

● An elderly woman wheelchair-user who still made beautiful and delicate lace on a cushion the way she had been taught by her mother so many years before. When her niece was getting married, she gave her some lace with which to trim the petti-coat beneath her wedding dress. This was seen by the maker of the wedding dress who was so impressed that she began commissioning yards of lace of different widths to be used on the gowns she made.

Of course, you may have no desire to earn money from your craft work. You may decide that you wish to create items purely for your own pleasure or to give as gifts. Whichever is the case, you should be able to derive a great deal of satisfaction from what you do – and developing a new skill or talent is always worth while.

Gardening

If you are someone who has always considered gardening to be back-breaking drudgery, you may wonder why I have included it in my list of 'talents'.

Apart from the fact that I believe there is a great deal of creativity involved in designing and developing a garden, there is so much you can do with what you grow.

- When sowing flower seeds for your own use, sow a few extra. These can be grown on in pots to be given as gifts, either individually or three or four in a bowl, perhaps with a matching ribbon.

- It is so easy to grow flowers for drying. These can then be used in arrangements, to decorate wall hangings, to make pictures or cards etc.

- Many plants and bulbs increase naturally in the garden and there comes a time when there just is not enough space for them all. The surplus can be potted up and given away or sold.

- You might like to try selling bunches of flowers or fresh herbs from your garden. You could do this through the Women's Institute market stalls, even if you are not a member of the WI. (See Chapter 10 for details.) You will never grow rich from such sales, but they might well help to pay for next year's seeds and bulbs.

- If you grow fruit and vegetables – particularly if they are grown organically – you will find that they are in great demand. These too can be sold through WI market stalls.

- You might like to turn your excess produce into home-made goods. Jams, jellies, vinegars and chutneys are always appreciated. Do remember, however, that there is no problem if you are giving these away but, should you decide to sell them, it is essential that you conform with such legislation as the Food Safety Act 1990, the Weights and Measures Act 1985 and regulations made thereunder. Full details and advice are obtainable at no charge from your Trading Standards Department (number in local telephone directory).

As well as selling or giving away what you grow in your garden, you might also have skills which are greatly in demand. There are many people who would appreciate having a beautiful garden, but do not have the knowledge or desire to create one. In addition, there are many elderly or infirm people who are no longer able to maintain their existing gardens and would be only too pleased if someone who knew what needed doing came along to help them.

Simon and Rachel were going through a very difficult time. They had only been married a few months when each of them was made redundant. Being young, neither of them had worked long enough to merit a large sum as redundancy payment. Money was obviously very tight and they had to struggle to make ends meet.

Both Simon and Rachel were keen gardeners but, now that they had plenty of 'spare' time, their small garden did not keep them occupied for long. They knew that Mr Elgood, an elderly man who lived a few doors away, had a large garden which he could no longer maintain so they offered to tend it for him. Having only his pension to live on, Mr Elgood could not afford to pay the young couple, but he offered them free use of a large portion of his garden as a vegetable plot – something they had no room for in their own tiny back garden.

Simon and Rachel were delighted. They created a flourishing vegetable garden, growing sufficient produce for their own use as well as for Mr Elgood's – and still having plenty left over to sell. Even when Simon eventually found another job, they were able to continue as all the hardest work – that of clearing the ground and setting out the garden – had already been done.

Whatever you decide to do and however you wish to make use of the time you have available while you are without a job, you may well find that you have far greater talents than you ever believed, and that you can develop and use these talents to enjoy yourself, to make friends and even to earn a little extra money.

7

The only way is up

You are a very lucky person! You may find that hard to believe as you try to put on a positive face while managing without a job – but it is true. Most people drift along through life never knowing whether the next few weeks are going to give them a lift or bring them down. You have been down – which may mean anything from bored or depressed to embarrassed and frightened. So for you the only way to go is up – and that knowledge makes you lucky. (Hopefully, if you have been working your way through this book, you have already started on that upward path but, believe me, there are even better times ahead.)

Have you ever stopped to think what it is you want from life? If, because of current circumstances, your instinctive answer is, 'a job', think again. A job – any old job – is not necessarily the only answer, although naturally the money it brings in would be a great help.

Most people, when questioned about what they want out of life, give the answer 'happiness'. But ask those same people to define what they mean by happiness and you will often find yourself confronted by blank looks. In this fast-paced and stress-filled world, most of us seem to spend so much time rushing from one crisis to another that we have very little awareness of how we are feeling at any given time.

Psychologist Mihaly Csikszentmihalyi tried to increase this awareness in the group of subjects with whom he was working. He attached to the clothes of each one a buzzer which would go off at random times during the day. Every time they heard the buzzer, the subjects had to stop and make a note of their feelings at the time, thus making them consciously aware of their emotions.

Perhaps, instead of talking about 'happiness', we should really be speaking of 'contentment' or 'fulfilment'. Happiness – a moment of pure joy – is a fleeting thing which touches you for just a moment before slipping away, while contentment is a continuous state. But, whichever word you choose to use, stop for a minute now and consider what it is that brings that emotion to you. Here are some of the answers given by a few of the people I interviewed on the subject:

- 'being needed';

- 'belonging – whether to a family or a community'.

- 'loving and being loved';

- 'looking at my baby';

- 'being busy';

- 'feeling confident';

- 'having enough money';

- 'time to myself to do what I enjoy just because I enjoy it';

- 'having something to aim for'.

Your definition will probably encompass most, if not all, of the above.

Having defined what happiness means to you, look through your list and see how many of the components are already present in your life. When it comes to those components that are missing, how many of them are within your control and can be achieved with a little effort on your part? You may find that you lack fewer of the essentials than you originally thought.

Contrasts are a valuable part of life. An object takes its shape and definition from the space around it; the spring and summer are all the more delightful after the chill of winter; and, although no one enjoys being sad, if there were no sadness, how would we know that we were happy? The fact that you have known the misery of being without a job when you would prefer to have one means that, as your life improves, you will be more capable of appreciating what it offers you than someone whose life has always been on an even keel.

You have only to think of the rich, the glamorous and the famous – those 'golden people' who appear to have no real worries. They can have everything they want – but are they necessarily happy? Of course it is wrong to generalise and I am positive that some of them are perfectly content with life – but think how many of them we read about who have turned to drink or drugs, run from one beautiful partner to another and even, in some cases, committed suicide. Were they truly happy? I think not.

In this chapter we are going to explore how you can set your life on a happier and more fulfilling path – whatever that means for you. But, until that point is reached, here are some instant 'happiness boosters' you can try.

- Think back to a moment in your life which made you happy – not with regret because it has passed, but with gladness and thankfulness that you were fortunate enough to experience it in the first place. If you have a photograph which helps to evoke the memory, look at it. If no such photograph exists, create a mental one. Close your eyes and see the situation as it was. Remember just how it felt and try to recreate that feeling now.

- Spoil yourself. Indulge in something which you love doing – just because you feel like it. It doesn't have to be an expensive pastime; you might like to soak in a perfumed bath, take the dog for a walk, listen to a favourite piece of music or spend time with a special friend.

- Breathe deeply. When someone is anxious or depressed their breathing becomes shallow and, taken to extremes, they begin to hyperventilate. Deep breathing – right from the diaphragm – induces a sense of well-being.

- Use affirmations. Whether you choose the basic 'every day in every way I am becoming happier' or decide to be more specific, positive affirmations have been shown to have a definite effect upon the subconscious and therefore upon the way you feel.

- Take some exercise. Whether it be a swim, a jog, a brisk walk – any of these will improve your circulation and direct more oxygen to the brain. This in turn will help you to feel uplifted and positive.

- Stand up straight – shoulders back, chin up – and smile! Really smile, with your mouth, your eyes and your heart. If you are with other people they will probably smile back – it's catching. If you are alone, I challenge you to do this and still feel depressed. Of course, if you could manage to laugh, that would be even better. In 1991 psychologist Robert Holden opened his Laughter Clinic in the Midlands and it has proved so effective that it is now NHS-financed.

The longer you find yourself in an unhappy state, the harder it becomes to do anything about it. Psychologically we are all resistant to change – even change for the better. Somehow the subconscious becomes used to the status quo and changes – particularly if you deliberately set out to make them – seem to cause it to feel uncomfortable. But if you persevere until you break through this discomfort barrier, your subconscious will soon become accustomed to a new set of feelings. It is not unlike wearing a new pair of shoes – they may be a little stiff at first, even if they are the right size. But, provided the quality is good, you will soon grow used to them and will accept them so that you cease thinking about whether or not they are comfortable.

In the same way, adjusting to change in your outlook and your way of thinking may take a little while, but it is well worth doing and you will soon become accustomed to the new you. Psychologists claim that it takes approximately three weeks to adjust to something new. If you want to prove this, try the following experiment. Take any object you use regularly and change its position, then see how long it takes before the new position becomes the accepted one. For example, if you have a waste-paper basket which has always stood to the right of your chair, move it to the left. For the first few days you will continue throwing bits of paper on the floor to your right, but it will not take very long for you to grow used to tossing them to the left.

If you have grown accustomed to thinking of yourself as unhappy with your current situation, you are going to have to work hard to change that inner view. You will need to remind yourself frequently – very frequently in those first days – that things can only get better, and that you are becoming happier and more positive with life. You might choose initially to use written or spoken affirmations to help you. But, as the days go by, you will find that you need these props less and less, and that you begin to feel more comfortable with the concept of a happier you.

You can look on all that has happened to you in two ways; you can think of it as a cruel blow dealt by fate – one which you have no choice but to submit to – or you can look on it as an opportunity to make some changes in the direction of your life. But this entails *doing* something. Of course you could just sit and wait for things to get better, but you could be in for a very long wait! How much better to grasp control of the situation and make a start. Of course, you might change your mind and your direction along the way – but at least you will have done something about taking control of your own life and destiny, and this is bound to make you feel better about yourself as a person. As we have already seen, the higher your self-esteem, the more you are prepared to do, so you will be setting out on a highly positive journey towards your future.

Try this little exercise: imagine you have just been told that you have precisely one year left to live. You are not going to be ill, not going to suffer in any way but, at the end of 12 months, you will exist no more. Given that situation, what would be the important things you would like to achieve in that time? Write them down.

Now suppose that, instead of 12 months, you have been given only six. You might not have time to do all the things on your original list, but which would be the most important – which ones do you feel you really want to achieve in the six months you have left? Write them down.

If you had only three months left you would have to refine your list still further. Do that now and write down what you feel you must do in those 12 or 13 weeks.

Suppose you have only one month to go – still with no pain, no discomfort and nothing preventing you doing whatever you wish, provided you can achieve it in the time. What would it be? Write it down.

If you had just a week left instead of a month, what would you do? And now contemplate the situation if you had just 24 hours to live. You would possibly only have time to put into action one thing. What would be the really important achievement in your last day?

Naturally I am not wishing you only another 24 hours of life – or even 12 months. But, if you work through this exercise honestly, it does help to focus the mind on that which is really important to you and to eliminate many of the trivial anxieties with which we all surround ourselves.

Setting goals

Whatever your current position, setting goals is essential if you are to progress at all. This applies to your working life as well as to your personal life and relationships. Creating a set of goals and progressing towards them not only helps in a practical sense; it gives you a feeling of taking control where perhaps you have felt in the past that life and circumstances have been the controllers, and you have been a victim, a mere pawn to be pushed from one square to the next.

The method of goal-setting which follows has been proved to work for many of my patients as well as for the business people with whom I have worked, especially those who have come to courses on coping with redundancy. Because it involves the use of your intuition as well as your logic, some people find it difficult at first. But it is well worth persevering, as it is helpful in clarifying the mind and pointing you in the right direction.

First select the area of your life with which you wish to deal – be it working or personal. Then proceed to each stage of the following goal-setting plan.

STAGE 1 LONG-TERM GOAL

For the purpose of this exercise, I am going to assume that 'long term' refers to a period of six years. However, you can adjust this time span to suit your own set of circumstances.

This section of the plan involves the greatest use of your intuition so, before proceeding to the actual task, promise yourself that you will give a completely spontaneous answer to the question asked. If you stop to consider possibilities and probabilities, to weigh up situations, to wonder if you are being foolish, you will put a block on the process and the whole exercise will be a waste of time.

Bearing that in mind, decide which area of your life you want to concentrate upon first – work, personal relationships etc. Once you have made that decision, and remembering that you must be spontaneous in your reply, give an instant answer to the following question: *What do you want to have achieved by six years from today?*

You may, of course, have been harbouring the same deep desire for the past 20 years. On the other hand, you may have been feeling that the one thing you really did not know was what you wanted. In either case, provided you really did answer the question instinctively rather than logically, your response probably indicates your subconscious wishes – and in some cases it may surprise you.

Write down your long-term aim and the date by which you intend to have achieved it (e.g. six years from today).

STAGE 2   MID-TERM GOAL

Once you have taken the time to reflect on your long-term goal and appreciate that, even if it did take you by surprise, it was a genuine indication of inner desires, you need to go on to consider your mid-term goal. If we are reckoning that 'long term' means six years, then mid term is three years.

This time use a combination of your intuition and your logical thought, trying to keep the balance between the two as equal as possible. Bearing your long-term goal in mind, *for your mid-term aim to be a real possibility, what will you have to achieve by three years from today?*

Once again, write down your answer.

STAGE 3   SHORT-TERM GOAL

For the purpose of this stage of the exercise you need to put from your mind your long-term goal. If it makes it easier, cover up the words you have written to describe it. Concentrate only on your answer to Stage 2 and your description of what you will have to achieve within the next three years.

Although, as in most areas of life, it is helpful to allow your instinct to play a part here, we are getting to the point where logic needs to take over more and more as you contemplate your replies to the questions. Keeping that in mind, please answer the following question: *If you are to achieve your mid-term goal in 3 years from now, what will you have to achieve within the next 12 months?*

As you write down your response, you will realise that you are getting closer and closer to a plan of action for your future.

STAGE 4   NEAR FUTURE GOAL

Now you have to put out of your mind your replies to Stages 1 and 2, and concentrate only upon what you wrote as your short-term goal. Using a greater degree of logic than instinct, answer this question: *If you are to have achieved your short-term goal by 12 months from now, what will you have to have done by three months from today?*

There may, in fact, be several things you will have to have done by three months' time if your short-term goal is to be attainable.

STAGE 5   IMMEDIATE ACTION

Bearing only your response to Stage 4 in mind and using your logic alone, answer this: *If you are to achieve your near future goal in three months, WHAT CAN YOU DO THIS WEEK?*

By now, because we have been refining the thought process with each stage, you should be able to think of something – however minor it might be – you can do within the next seven days which will help you towards your near future goal. Then of course, it is up to you to do it.

Putting this plan into action at the first possible moment will bring two great benefits; first, you will truly have taken the first step towards achieving one of your life goals and, secondly, you will realise that you are now really in control of your life. This realisation will not only boost your self-esteem – it will also engender a sense of excitement as you realise that you are about to embark on a definite plan of campaign.

GOAL SHEETS

To show you how well this system works, I am going to reproduce the goal sheets completed by two of the young people I worked with in a recent television series. The first, whom I shall call Judy, was at the time 22 years old. She had been married to Tom for just over a year and she worked in the personnel department of a large manufacturing company. Here is Judy's goal sheet:

What would you like to have achieved by six years from today?

I want to be at home looking after a family.

In order to achieve that, what stage will you have to reach by three years from today?

Apart from possibly having one or more babies, I will have to be earning enough money to save some so that I can afford to leave work.

To have reached that stage in three years' time, what will you have to have done by 12 months from today?

I will have to have been promoted within the department as higher grades command much higher salaries and I would be able to save.

If that is what you need to do by 12 months from now, what must you do within the next three months?

I must begin studying to gain my promotion.

What can you do next week?

I can find out about available courses and exams, and start to work out which path I am to follow.

The second example is that of a young man whom I shall call Peter. He had been working for a builders' supply merchant and, as a result of the recession and the slump in the building trade, at the age of 24 had just been made redundant. When I first met him he was quite depressed and did not really know what he wanted to do. Here is his goal sheet.

What would you like to have achieved by six years from today?

I would like to be on a career path with prospects rather than in a dead-end job.

In order to achieve that, what stage will you have to have reached by three years from today?

I will have to be employed in a job which has the potential to take me further up the ladder.

To reach that stage by three years' time, what will you have to have done by 12 months from today?

I will have to be retrained or be in the process of doing so.

If that is what you need to do by 12 months from now, what must you do within the next three months?

To decide upon the direction I want to take and to have started my training.

What can you do next week?

Arrange a meeting with a careers adviser, find out what courses are available at the local college of further education and gather any literature which might be helpful.

Peter finally decided upon a career in the computer world and is now part-way through a course for which he was given a career development loan.

THE NEXT STEP

Such a goal sheet will not necessarily provide the final and definitive answer to all your problems, but it should help to focus your mind on the next step to take. Even if you decide as you progress that you are not happy with the path you have chosen, you will have taken some steps to help yourself achieve your aims. Over many years of working with people who are trying to discover a sense of direction, I have found that – provided sufficient use of intuition was involved in answering the first question – in most cases the path chosen has proved to be a satisfactory one.

Naturally you may not be able to adhere strictly to the times given. Peter could find that some courses take longer than others, while it might take Judy longer than she expected to become pregnant. But with a little adaptation the answers and the stages on the goal sheet would still remain the same.

Additionally, of course, there are times when life seems to throw one obstacle after another in your path and your way ahead may not be as clear-cut as you originally hoped. But there are always methods of overcoming obstacles and you may simply have to take a slightly different route in the achievement of your goals. This should not prove too great a problem, although it may necessitate some rethinking or even the creation of a new goal sheet. After all, if you set out to travel from point A to point B and on the way you find that your usual route has been blocked by a fallen tree, you do not give in and return home. No, you turn around and take a different path – even if it happens to be a slightly longer one – and continue until you reach your intended destination.

It is also a good idea to stop and take stock of the situation every now and then along the way. Ask yourself whether things are progressing as you hoped they would, whether you are still on the right path towards these goals or whether – perhaps in the light of your increased knowledge – it would be preferable to make some adjustments to the original plan. This sometimes happens when you discover possibilities you had never even realised until you started on your journey towards your goals.

When I left school I decided that I wanted a career using modern languages and so I went to a college to study these. As one of the extra subjects, at that college we were also taught to stenotype. This involved using manually operated machines not unlike those you see in films of American courtroom scenes. I found that not only did I thoroughly enjoy stenotyping, but I was also very good at it and, although I completed the course, the use of foreign languages became less important to me as I focused my attention on a career as a stenotypist (we were called 'shorthandwriters' even though we did not use shorthand) in the British law courts. Even had I been compiling a goal sheet in those days, there was no way in which I could have stated that my aim was to become a stenotypist because I did not even know such a thing existed; it was something I discovered along the way.

Setting goals and working towards them is not only useful – it is also exciting. It helps to rekindle feelings of optimism and positivity which can so easily become lost when we feel depressed or without hope because we are without a job.

Imagination

You have already seen that, for your goal-setting technique to work effectively, you need to use both your logic and your intuition. You can also employ another great tool – your imagination.

Imagination is highly underrated in this left-brained, logical world of ours where it is frequently thought that, if one is to succeed, cold, clear thought is the only answer. Of course it is *part* of the answer, but some of the most significant names in the world of business, science and invention have become great because they knew how to combine practicality with a little daydreaming – feet on the ground with castles in the air.

Many of the great inventors and innovators have told of the way in which they used their imagination and their subconscious mind in the creation of their most significant ideas. Thomas Edison claimed that, when faced with a difficult problem during the course of the inventive process, he would go to bed at night and spend some moments considering the particular question which was troubling him. He would not even attempt to work out the answer, but would just mentally pose the question to himself. He repeated this process each night until one morning – usually after no more than three or four days at the most – he awoke either knowing the solution or the method of discovering it.

Children are naturally imaginative. Their world knows no boundaries. Think of all those invisible 'friends' they seem to have. And adults feed this imagination with stories of magic, talking toys and fairies. Then, suddenly, these same children find themselves at school where – unless they are particularly fortunate – imagination becomes a thing of the past and they are urged to 'think', 'learn', 'concentrate' and to 'stop daydreaming'.

In many ways, the more affluent society becomes, the more difficult we make it for our children to develop their imaginative ability. When many toys were home-made, the same blank-faced rag doll could be adult, child, fairy or witch. Today's dolls seem to come not only with complete wardrobes, but also with names and characters which prohibit the variety of wonderland voyages yesterday's child could experience.

The artist faced with a blank canvas, the sculptor standing before a piece of cold, hard stone, the inventor who knows what he wants to achieve, but has to discover *how* to do it – all these people have to use their powers of imagination before they begin to employ the practical application of their technical skills. You have practical skills and abilities too, but it is often only by means of using your imagination that you will discover the best way to employ them.

Don't just wait for inspiration to strike. We all seem to get caught up in so many tasks and commitments that the time will never be right. If you want to use your imagination to help you, you need to set aside a regular period of time for its development. You don't need to spend hours doing this – even 10 or 15 minutes a day will be enough. It is regularity of endeavour which is important.

Here is a technique for developing the use of your imagination and its access to your subconscious mind. You may not wish to use it to create a work of art, to change the world or to have a lasting influence on society. Perhaps all you desire is to make some improvement in your own life. The system will still work for you too.

1 As with any exercise where instinct, intuition and the subconscious mind are involved, it is necessary first to relax as completely as possible. You may wish to sit in a comfortable chair or you may prefer to lie down. Then close your eyes and, starting with your feet and working upwards, tense and relax each set of muscles in turn, ending with those around the head, jaw and neck.

2 Spend a few moments listening to the steady rhythm of your own breathing and ensuring that your limbs feel as heavy as possible.

3 Next, concentrate on the problem before you at the time – and it doesn't matter whether it is great or small; if it is bothering you, it is a problem. You could mentally ask a question or you might prefer to visualise your problem. Don't at this point attempt to come up with a solution.

4 Now it is time to allow your imagination to take flight. See how many different trains of thought are triggered off by the

problem. Don't only concentrate on sane and sensible ideas – the more fanciful (even ridiculous) your thoughts, the better. If you are unaccustomed to using your imagination in this way, you might well find this process awkward or difficult to begin with – but persevere, it does get easier. If you are really stuck, you could try asking yourself the question 'What if' and allowing a series of images to come into your mind.

5 When you run out of ideas, open your eyes and make a note of as many as you can remember – being sure to write down the ridiculous along with the sensible, as it is often those that seem far-fetched at first which finally end up by providing the best solution.

6 Read and re-read your notes. You will find that from all those improbable and implausible solutions, the answer you require will appear to stand out. And it may be nothing like the same answer you would have come up with by means of logical thought alone.

If this concept is completely new to you, you may find yourself having to repeat the process over several days before anything at all seems to come into your mind. This should not worry you as, with a little practice, it will soon become easier.

You may be thinking to yourself that this technique cannot possibly work – or you may think you will feel foolish doing it. But pause for a moment and ask yourself why so many businesses hold brainstorming sessions which are designed to allow *all* ideas to be thrown into the thinking-pot, with any serious consideration of these ideas taking place only at the end. They do it because it *works*. Some of the ideas to emerge from such brainstorming sessions include the games tables for small children to be found in many banks and building societies, the lap-top computer, taking pets to visit the residents of old people's homes, and selling 'shares' in horses, donkeys and ponies to help with the maintenance and upkeep of a sanctuary designed to protect them.

Imagination alone is obviously not the answer. In fact, using imagination which has not been coloured and possibly modified by common sense could cause problems. As psychologist Caroline Hall says: 'We can imagine what it is like to fly but we can't fly. You need to understand what imagination is and use it wisely.'

You have looked at goal setting and what you want to achieve. You have remembered what it is like to be a success at something. Now use your imagination in another positive way by taking that goal and imagining that you have already attained it. Go on, close your eyes and *see* yourself having already reached that goal. Imagine what it would feel like to know that you have done so. This is just what athletes like Linford Christie are doing just before the start of an important race. They are 'seeing' the race as over and themselves as winners. And it works.

If these methods succeed for the business executives and the athletes, there is no reason why they should not succeed for you. It may take practice; it may involve a new way of thinking; it will definitely be worth while.

8

Don't just sit there

Being without a job can cause many different reactions, but by far the most prevalent is the tendency to do nothing. This is particularly true when the individual is faced with the crisis situation of suddenly losing their job – and it applies even if there were 'advance signals' that this might be the case. These days people are so used to the threat of redundancy hanging over an entire work force that there is usually a tendency to think that it will not happen to you. And, even if a company has a retirement policy which states that everyone will leave at the age of 55, many people either believe that the policy will change before they reach that age or that an exception will be made in their case. So the shock, when it comes, can be quite devastating.

Of course, in some instances there is no warning at all. There are far too many stories of people going to work as usual, believing that everything is fine, only to find that day to be their last working day and that suddenly they are jobless with little more than a month's salary to take home, plus the promise of a redundancy payment which, even if it appears generous at first glance, will certainly not keep a family for the foreseeable future.

No wonder we think of these as crisis situations and no wonder we react to them as we do to all other crises in our lives – by being

frozen into inactivity. When faced with other crises, however –
illness, accident, fire etc – the urgent need for immediate action
curtails this inactivity and we are forced to cope in whatever is
the most appropriate way. Because loss of a job, however distressing, does not appear to require *immediate* action, it is easy
for that period of inactivity to be prolonged until it becomes a
habit – at which point it is really difficult to do anything about it.

For someone who has never been able to get a job in the first
place, however many attempts have been made, it is not unusual
for the initial effort and enthusiasm to wane, and for apathy to
set in. One young female university graduate I spoke to told me
that she had written over 200 letters of application before she
was granted her first interview. Of course this is disheartening,
and it is easy to understand how it becomes more and more
difficult to make the effort when every door appears to be shut.
This is even more the case when the unsuccessful applicant
believes (correctly or not) that everyone else considers them to
be a layabout who does not want to work but is happy to 'live off
the State'.

We have already seen that any state of mind can be habit-
forming, so that changing it can take quite an effort and can even
be uncomfortable. So it is important to get hold of feelings of
inertia or boredom before they become a way of life and destroy
your self-esteem completely.

Let's look at some of the different groups of people doing their
best to survive without a job, and see how each can do as much as
possible to boost their enthusiasm and their confidence.

Young unemployed

It is no longer the case that there is a job waiting for every
school-leaver so some, even those with good exam results or
specific skills, find themselves trying in vain to break into the

employment market. Others either have to make do with menial work or drift unhappily from one dead-end job to another simply to ensure that some money comes in.

Money is, of course, a big problem. While the school-leaver may not have a mortgage to pay or a family to support, neither do they have the means in many cases to find the deposit and advance payment usually needed in order to rent accommodation. This means that, for many, the only answer is to remain at home with parents at an age when they would previously have expected to be independent. Naturally this does nothing to enhance the self-esteem.

One of the major problems young people face when completing job application forms is that all potential employers seem to be asking for details of 'previous experience'. As a young man called Danny put it, 'How are we supposed to gain experience if no one will give us a job in the first place? But if we don't have it, no one wants to take us on.'

The solution is to try and find some other way of gaining the type of experience which would single you out from a crowd of applicants, and make you attractive to a potential employer. The type of experience will naturally vary according to your practical aptitudes and academic abilities, but there are many things you can do, on a voluntary basis, which would give you a chance to prove yourself and to convince a future employer of your value.

Tony was a skilled worker with wood and had a strong sense of design but, although he had had a couple of temporary jobs, he had been unable to find any work which used his talents. To counteract his boredom and disillusionment while searching for a job, he offered his services to the local amateur dramatic society as a painter and builder of scenery. He was made very welcome by the members of the society and, when it became obvious that he was extremely good at what he was doing, Tony was asked to design some of the sets for the next production. This he did and they were such a success that photographs were taken of them, and the local newspaper even wrote a short piece on Tony and his work.

Some time after this a job became available with a company designing and making individually crafted items of furniture. Tony decided that this would be just right for him and filled out an application form. When it came to the section asking about 'experience', he was able to submit photographs, cuttings and letters of recommendation from members of the dramatic society – some of whom were quite prominent local figures. Although he had not been paid for his efforts – and had not even undertaken it as a means to finding work – Tony discovered that he now had the necessary experience and he was given the job.

Lucy did not really know what sort of job she wanted. She had basic commercial skills, and a lively and intelligent mind but, apart from knowing that she wanted to work in the world of business, she had no real sense of direction. This caused her to feel unsure of herself and, although she went for a few interviews, her lack of confidence made her awkward and unable to do herself justice.

For several years Lucy had helped out during the school holidays and at weekends at a local animal sanctuary. She used to feed and exercise the animals, and, as she put it, 'give them a bit of love'. Finding herself with too much time on her hands, she went to the director of the sanctuary to ask for more voluntary work. She was told that the sanctuary was in danger of closing because funds were so low that they could no longer afford to support all the animals while paying essential bills. Not being able to bear the thought of all those defenceless animals being made homeless or, worse still, destroyed, Lucy grew determined. She was going to do something about it. At that point she did not know *what* she was going to to, but she would not allow the sanctuary to shut down through lack of money.

She and her friends had a brainstorming session, tossing ideas – both sensible and ridiculous – around until they came up with a solution which satisfied Lucy. Raffles and fundraising activities such as jumble sales or treasure hunts were all very well, but the amount they raised was often minimal and was soon used up. What they needed was ongoing commitment from people but, with Britain in recession, no one was able to afford to promise large sums of money. So Lucy decided to sell shares in the animals. She organised a campaign whereby many people would each be asked to donate a small but regular sum towards the upkeep of whichever animal or breed they chose. They would receive a certificate with a picture of 'their' animal and would be kept informed of its condition by means of a quarterly newsletter.

The response from the public was overwhelming. Many people were anxious to help, but had felt unable to offer the large sums of money they thought would be needed. But a small, regular amount was a different matter – particularly when they felt that they were playing a part in the care of a specific creature. The scheme worked and, although by no means affluent, the sanctuary was able to remain open and continue its worthwhile efforts.

Now Lucy had something to write about when asked for her 'previous experience'. In addition, she had discovered that she possessed organisational abilities she never knew about and her self-confidence had increased enormously. She knew she had to look for a job where she would eventually be able to make use of her particular talents. She finally found work as an assistant in the marketing department of a national organisation where she was able increasingly to use her skills and abilities.

Becoming involved in activities other than job-hunting can prove to be valuable in so many ways. We have already seen how it can give a boost to your CV or to an application form. But, apart from that, it also gives you a sense of purpose, and a means of meeting and being involved with a whole new group of people as well as, in many cases, the sense of achievement which accompanies the knowledge that you are doing something worth while.

Looking for work can be an expensive business. The cost of postage, telephone calls and travelling soon mounts up – and all this at a time when your finances are likely to be at a very low ebb. Don't be shy of making use of the Job Clubs which exist to help you at such times. Not only will you receive advice on the best way to apply for a job or complete a CV, you will also have access to telephones, stationery and postage stamps. In some cases the company to whom you apply will refund your travel costs; in others you may be able to receive help from the Job Club or Department of Social Security.

—— *Victims of redundancy* ——

Not unnaturally you may well find yourself feeling numb as a result of the trauma of redundancy. And, as we saw at the beginning of this book, it is worth taking a little time to deal with the tangle of emotions within you, and acknowledging precisely how you feel and why. But, having done all that, there comes a point where you have to make a firm decision – are you going to collapse in a heap under the weight of redundancy or are you going to get out there and do something about it?

This is not another way of saying 'Snap out of it' – I wouldn't dream of being so insensitive. What I am saying is that there is life after redundancy, even if it is not the life you previously thought you were aiming for. I can call to mind a considerable number of people I have met – either as individual clients or on one of my redundancy courses – who are now working again in a way which brings them more satisfaction (and often more money) than ever before. And this does not apply to young people only; many of those who were made redundant at the age of 50 or over and who thought that their working life had come to an end are now finding fulfilment in work once more.

Although many employers still seem to consider being 55 as synonymous with being well over the hill, that view is gradually beginning to change. Indeed, in the future it will have to as there has been a decline in the number of school-leavers since the late 1970s, while the number of people over 55 is increasing. Changes in population indicate that this pattern will continue for some time to come. It is for this reason, among others, that Dow-Stoker, the training specialists, devised a returners' programme which is sponsored by several well-known names in the retail world – among them Tesco, B&Q and Thorn EMI. These companies make a point of employing mature staff, and claim that the older worker is often more conscientious and better at dealing with members of the public.

Whatever your age, the first thing to do after the shock of redundancy has subsided is to take stock of yourself and your situation. If you are to seek further employment you will need an up-to-date CV and this should be prepared with care – and with specialist help if you feel unable to tackle it yourself. The first impression a possible future employer will have of you will be your CV, so it is worth taking the time and trouble to make it not only accurate but attractive too.

Although the tendency is to do otherwise, make sure you tell everyone that you have been made redundant. It is sadly a common occurrence, so no one will look down on you for this. You would be surprised at how many new job opportunities come through personal contacts – but if they don't know you are looking, how can they help? It is worth sitting down and listing all your possible contacts – personal and business – and getting in touch with them. Research shows that 50 per cent of all executives obtain jobs through this sort of networking so it is well worth doing.

Treat looking for a job as a day's work. It is so easy to say that you will tackle it after you have done the shopping or cut the grass but, if you are serious about finding employment, you will have to put in some effort. Obviously you can read newspapers (and specific trade journals if applicable) to look for jobs. *Executive Post* can be obtained free from Job Centres for graduates and those of middle and senior management level. Write letters, make telephone calls – in fact, treat the whole thing as a business project. It is often better if you can find somewhere other than your home in which to do all this – reference libraries are good places to work, and staff are usually very helpful when it comes to details of organisations, agencies and specific periodicals.

Of course, you may decide that you have had enough of being an employee with all the attendant risks of finding yourself without a job through no fault of your own. Perhaps this is the time to think about becoming self-employed. Indeed, perhaps this was just the push you needed.

Jack had worked for a large commercial photographic agency for over 20 years when two things happened. First the recession struck, reducing the company's income; secondly the nephew of the managing director was looking for a job and his uncle decided to take him into the firm. This meant that someone else had to go – and the unfortunate victim was Jack.

For some years Jack had been thinking about setting up his own company, though on a smaller scale than his former employers and dealing with a select group of clients with specialised needs. He had the skill and the experience needed. He did not have all the money, but would probably have been able to obtain finance had he tried. What he did not have was the courage to break away from the monthly salary and take a chance. Now the choice had been made for him. The monthly salary no longer existed but, after such long service, his redundancy payment was substantial. After discussing the matter with his wife and with professional advisers, Jack decided that this was the perfect opportunity to show what he could do and form his own company. This he did, and went on to be happier and more fulfilled than ever before, with an income which eventually, after two or three years, was greater than his former salary.

For some people self-employment would not be the answer. If you feel more comfortable within the structure of a large organisation, and would become weighed down and stressed by the responsibilities of running your own business, then obviously you should be looking for a job. But many people enjoy the sense of freedom and the flexibility of being their own boss, and can cope with the sudden deadlines which involve working all hours. For these people, self-employment is ideal.

Running your own business does not have to mean setting up some vast multinational organisation. Indeed, many successful businesses are single-person businesses and begin by being based in the home of the individual concerned. (If you decide to follow this path, do remember that you may need to make some alterations to your home insurance.) Many skills can be used successfully as the basis for a home-run business – from dressmaking and crafts to typing and desk-top publishing.

If you decide to set up a home-based business, you will have to do the thing properly and not treat it as an extension of your hobby. A good way to start is by paying a visit to your local Training and Enterprise Council (TEC); you will be given free advice and, in many cases, free training in basic business skills. You will also receive help in preparing a business plan which you will need to show your bank manager. In addition, your TEC will give you information about grants, career development loans and other possible means of financial assistance. Details vary from year to year and from area to area, so contact your local TEC for up-to-date information.

When Alison was made redundant by the public relations company for whom she had worked, she decided to turn disaster into opportunity and set up in business for herself. She already had a good word processor at home, so she invested in a state-of-the-art printer and advertised her services as a typist of everything from individual letters to theses and even books. She had expected business to be slow at first and was amazed at the response she had to her relatively inexpensive advertisements. She soon had more work than she could comfortably handle; she also calculated that, even were she to work every hour of every day, there was a finite amount of money to be made. So she recruited other women who were based at home for various reasons – they had young children, were not able to find work or did not want to be tied down to the specific demands of an outside job. Alison was able to concentrate on the organisational side of the business, keeping only a small amount of the more interesting jobs for herself; the rest she passed on to her team of typists. She paid them well, retaining a proportion of the fee as her commission and, of course, she herself was ultimately responsible for the final checking of the work. Soon, almost without intending it to happen, she found she had a thriving business on her hands.

———— *Women returners* ————

Not so very many years ago, once a woman married – and certainly once she had children – that was usually the end of her going out to work. Then came the time when women began to ask themselves whether or not they should return to work. Now, of course, they ask themselves *when* they should return. And it is not just because they want the money – although no one is denying that it is useful and sometimes essential. Women can now acknowledge that they seek a sense of fulfilment as individuals and to many of them this involves a career – or at least a job.

Deciding to return to work is just the beginning. This is where the problems start. If you have children you have to arrange for them to be looked after or else hope to find a job which entails you working only specific hours. Such jobs are available, but they tend to be at the lower end of the employment market in terms of pay and opportunity. While such a small number of companies have any child-care facilities, if you are intent on pursuing a career you have to find reliable people to look after your children, whether they are babies needing day-long care or at school and in need of someone to look after them at the end of the day and during the holidays.

Even supposing you have solved all those problems – or perhaps you are a mother who wishes to return to work now that your children have all left home – where do you begin? You may have been away from the world of employment for so long that you do not know where to begin. And, unfortunately, the longer the gap in your working life, the less confidence you are likely to have in yourself. Marie, a mother in her 40s who had chosen to remain at home to look after her three children told me, 'I left as a shorthand typist. Since then a whole new world has grown up – computers, fax machines, modems, printers . . . I just wouldn't know where to start.'

Of course there are courses you can go on which will teach you how to use modern technology, but they don't necessarily do a great deal for your confidence. When Marie left work she knew she was good at her job and in control of the situation. Now, even with basic training in technological skills, she felt very much the 'new girl' – someone who had to start at the bottom of the ladder again.

A number of the more enlightened companies, such as Nat-West Bank, Unilever and Esso, now allow you to keep in touch with office life while at home looking after your children for up to five years by means of newsletters and seminars. They then promise not to penalise you for taking that break, allowing you to return at your former level, provided you undertake some essential updating in training when you come back. The head of staff relations at Esso, for example, said: '[The scheme] is open to all our employees at all levels. They can take up to five years' leave and come back to a guaranteed job providing they've been a satisfactory employee of the company for at least a year.'

Your local TEC should also be able to give you information about returners' courses in your area. These courses are designed to help women make decisions about the direction they would like their future career to take, and also help them prepare a suitable CV and practise interview techniques. Quite apart from these skills, they do a great deal to boost the self-esteem as confidence grows week by week.

One of the greatest problems facing women returners seems to be the tendency to under-sell and under-value themselves. Of course this is a generalisation and, as ever, there are exception, but this tends to be more of a feminine trait than a masculine one. Rennie Fritchie, experienced in wage negotiation, says, 'Women tend to think of a number, halve it and take away the first number they thought of. That's what they ask for.'

True or not, in 1990 British women were still earning an average of 25 per cent less than men in similar jobs. To some extent this is because they are unwilling to fight for equal financial rights. And, if women sell themselves short, is it any wonder that many companies do the same? This was proved by one organisation which, a couple of years ago, advertised a specific position at £20,000 a year. The advertisement was written in such a way that it would appeal to either sex and yet almost every applicant was a man. As an experiment, the same advertisement appeared offering a salary of £14,000; this time more than half the applicants were women. There seemed to be a mental price barrier for the women; if the salary was higher, the job must be beyond them.

And yet the skills used in running a home and bringing up a family are just those managerial skills so eagerly sought in the work place. They include personnel development, communication skills, time management, financial planning, leadership skills, assertiveness techniques and any number of practical abilities. But ask some women what they have been doing for the last few years and they will say things like 'just a housewife', 'only bringing up the children' or 'nothing much, just running a playgroup'.

If you are going for an interview, find out what the going rate is for the type of work you hope to be doing and don't expect to be paid less – except perhaps during an initial training period. Make sure you know what the potential career prospects are; don't be afraid to ask. The best interviewee is the one who is assertive and confident, and who appears to be aware of the current situation.

Prepare well for the interview. In addition to finding out what you can about the organisation concerned, make a list of the qualities you have to offer the company so that you will be able to state them when the time comes. Don't be afraid to discuss money; there is no point in taking a job which will just about pay your overheads – you might as well stay at home and potter.

When planning a return to work, it is vital that you remain assertive and learn to value yourself. After all, if you don't, how can you expect other people to?

Retired

Attitude plays a great part in your enjoyment (or otherwise) of your retirement. For some it is a delightful chance to spend more time indulging in all those hobbies which used to be fitted in at the end of a working day. Others view it as a stagnant time, an empty period in their lives; they see it as a 'running down' period and think of themselves as old and 'past it', even though 65 is no longer considered old – and many people retire before reaching this age.

In an ideal world we would all start planning for our retirement in our mid 30s or even earlier. We would make every effort to keep ourselves as fit as possible so that we would be able to maintain our health; we would develop interests unconnected with our work so that we looked forward to retirement as a positive and fulfilling time. Unfortunately human nature does not always work that way and the most we tend to do is consider some sort of pension plan to take care of our financial needs in later life. Surely our other needs are important too?

Even if you have done nothing in the way of forward planning for your retirement, there is a great big interesting world out there just waiting for you to join it. There are groups and clubs covering almost every subject under the sun, so you will be bound to find at least one to interest you. Details of these are usually available at your local library.

You could become more involved in your local community. There may be a residents' association in your area or a Neighbourhood Watch scheme; now that you have more time to spare, you could be invaluable to them, and it would give you a chance to speak up on behalf of yourself and others.

Whatever your previous educational experience, now is the chance to learn something just because you want to and not because it will help in your career. From cordon bleu to calligraphy, Polish to pottery, there are classes to be found in just about every subject – and there are usually concessionary rates for those who are retired. Perhaps you wish to take learning a stage further and study for a degree. More and more universities are accepting mature students, some of whom are well into their 70s and most of whom are eligible for a grant. If you would rather learn at your own pace and in your own home, you could take an Open University degree. If you are not too concerned about final qualifications, you could study with the University of the Third Age which does not demand any specific qualifications for acceptance, but does not give any on completion.

Learning helps to keep the mind alert and the brain active, so that the loss of memory which used always to be associated with increasing age need not occur. It also helps to maintain a lively and positive attitude towards life which can prevent the onset of retirement-induced psychological problems. It has also been found that older students often learn far better than younger ones – perhaps because they are more motivated or less pressured, or perhaps because they have a broader experience of life into which the newly acquired learning can be assimilated.

If you really find that you miss the routine of work and – particularly if you live alone – the companionship you once knew, it should be possible to find a part-time job, whether paid or voluntary. Many companies are now recruiting older staff for part-time work and voluntary organisations are always on the look-out for willing helpers. Whether you work in a charity shop, sell raffle tickets or join a fund-raising committee, your time and experience will be valued, and you will have the pleasure of knowing that what you are doing is helping others in some way.

Even if joints become a little stiffer or eyesight a little weaker, you should still be able to enjoy former hobbies. They may just need a little adapting to suit your current needs. Flower beds can be raised to reduce the need for bending, strong lighting and magnifying glasses can help with close work from crochet to painting, 9 holes of golf can be as enjoyable as 18, and the marathon runner of yesterday can become the rambler of today.

Many people approaching retirement age grow anxious as they consider the possible onset of failing health. But, as we have seen, less than 4 per cent of 65 year olds are in hospital and the figure only rises at 85.

This does not mean, of course, that you should not do everything within your power to maintain your health. It is as important as ever to eat as great a variety of food as possible to ensure an adequate intake of vitamins and minerals. It is also important to drink at least three pints of liquid a day – which can include fruit juices and even soups. Lack of fluid can cause headaches and fatigue – even poor balance and, in extreme cases, mental confusion.

Exercise is vital too if you are to remain healthy and here you have a great advantage. If you decide you want to swim, or attend a local sports or leisure centre, you will usually find that there are special reduced rates for those who can attend in off-peak times. You might also be able to take advantage of out-of-season holiday offers and set off to find some winter sunshine. Apart from being enjoyable, sunlight (and you don't have to sunbathe to get the benefit) gives you vitamins A and D, the latter being the one to help in the prevention of osteoporosis. There are now many organisations which specialise in holidays for the retired – some of them extremely active – so that you can also enjoy the company of others and perhaps make new friends if you are on your own.

Whatever group you belong to – or even if you do not really fit into any of the categories mentioned – you will feel so much better in yourself if you go ahead and do something rather than sit back and wait for things to improve. Just a few of the benefits waiting for you are:

- a chance to do something you have always wanted to do;

- the opportunity to meet new people of all ages;

- a way of helping others;

- a sense of optimism and a reason to look forward to the future;

- increased self-assurance;

- improved mental and physical health.

The more you do, the more confident you will become. And self-confidence *shows*. It will be apparent to everyone – friends, relatives, prospective employers – and, most important of all, to you. You will feel that you have a sense of purpose, even if you do not have a job and, as your self-esteem increases, you will come to believe that you can achieve whatever you wish – be it a new job, a chance to set up in business for yourself or a long and happy retirement.

9

Team work

We all need other people in our lives: we like to share our good times with them and our problems when things are not going so well. From the moment we are born most of us are surrounded by other people – first the family and then the school, college, work place, neighbours, those with whom we share particular hobbies or interests and so on.

Although it is the worst possible time for you to feel isolated, there may be many reasons why finding yourself without a job makes it difficult for you to mix with other people.

Young unemployed

The young unemployed have left their school or college companions behind; some will, in fact, have moved away while others are preoccupied with their own lives and their own problems. And the place where, at one time, you would have met new people, found new friends, taken up new activities – the work place – does not yet exist for you. So you find yourself in some sort of limbo where, unless you take active steps to do something about it, you could withdraw further and further into an isolated world.

This sense of isolation is emphasised if you see your former friends and co-students getting jobs before you do. Logic plays no part in the way you feel when this happens. You know and I know that ability, perseverance and attitude – and a certain amount of luck – are important when it comes to getting a job these days but, if you are already feeling negative, it is easy to convince yourself that everyone else is finding a job because they are all so much better than you are. Start to believe that and you will soon stop trying altogether.

Because money is in short supply at this stage in your life, you may not be able to go out very often – thus eliminating yet another point of social contact. Clubs, pubs, restaurants and discos all cost money, as do theatres and cinemas. Even taking part in sporting activities may involve the purchase of special equipment. It is all too easy to give up outings altogether rather than go along and find yourself the one who cannot afford to join in.

Redundancy

The shock to the system of being made redundant will often cause the person concerned to withdraw from everyone in the short term. This even applies to friends and family who may be truly sympathetic and understanding. It is not what is being said and thought which has this effect, but what the individual *imagines* is being said and thought. The person may feel that he or she has let everyone down or has shown that he or she is less able or worthy than other people.

Quite often, particularly if the threat of redundancy has been hanging over the company for some time, you will have worked extra hard and put in extra hours trying to fend off the dreaded day. This might mean that you have given up many social activities which you previously enjoyed; there may have been little time for squash, dinner parties or football when it seemed as though your job was at stake. Once one has been cutting down on that type of thing, it is quite difficult to pick up the threads again. This is even more the case if you feel (however misguidedly) that you now carry with you some sort of social stigma.

And, of course, money has suddenly become more of an issue for you too. Even if you have received a handsome redundancy payment, you are not quite sure how long it will have to last you. And, if you have a mortgage to pay and a family to feed, this can be a tremendous source of concern. One of the first things you are likely to do, therefore, is cut back the amount you spend on social activities.

Women returners

For the woman who has spent time at home looking after a family – whether we are talking about 5 years or 15 – it is really a case of starting again. Life with young children is extremely time-consuming and days fly by in a mist of practicalities. Suddenly – or so it appears – those children have grown and have either left home or are now so involved in their own activities that they no longer need you in quite the same way. You may well have lost touch with any former colleagues, and the other mothers you came to know through playgroups and schools might be looking to broaden their own horizons. (And, anyway, you might discover that you have nothing much in common with them other than the fact that you have children of a similar age.)

Starting again at this stage can be quite daunting. Gone is the confidence of youth; you may be less sure of your skills and abilities, and, as you look around you it often appears that everyone else has much to do and so many places to rush to that you wonder just how you are going to clamber on to this non-stop merry-go-round to take your turn.

Retirement

The psychological effect of retirement is well chronicled. No matter how well you feel, no matter what anyone tells you to the contrary, it is – certainly initially – quite difficult to avoid the thought that your time of usefulness is over. Of course we all know that this is not the case, but that does not prevent those feelings arising.

It has also been established that one of the worst things to do when you retire is suddenly to move away from your home. The cottage in the country or the apartment by the sea sound so tempting but, unless you already know people in the area, you can find yourself feeling very isolated. Making new friends is often more difficult as you grow older – particularly for a retired couple who tend to spend a great deal of their time together.

Take the example of Max and Doreen who were really looking forward to their retirement. They had so many plans. Doreen worked part-time until she was 62, just a couple of months before Max's 65th birthday. They had already decided that, as soon as they had both left work, they would look for a bungalow on the south coast – an area of the country they both loved and which they had visited many times on holiday. A few months after Max's retirement they found their dream home and were able to move in just after Christmas.

Neither Max nor Doreen knew anyone in the area of their new home, but this did not bother them. They told themselves that they would spend a few months settling in and familiarising themselves with the district. By then it would be almost summer, and they knew that both their children with their respective families would be happy to come and visit them. When autumn came, they told each other, they would find out about joining the local bridge club and the horticultural society. Each of them was fit and active, and they envisaged a long and happy retirement in their new-found home.

Then, in early March, tragedy struck. Max was struck by a car when crossing the road and critically injured. He was taken to the local hospital where he died a few days later. Doreen was naturally devastated. She went to stay with her married daughter for a few weeks and, when she returned to the bungalow, the same daughter came with her and stayed to look after her mother for a fortnight. Eventually, however, she had to return home to the north of England to take care of her own family.

It was only at this time that Doreen realised she knew no one at all in the vicinity of her new home. Until that moment she had spent all her time with loving members of her family, but now she had no one at all to talk to. If she went into the local shops no one knew her. If she walked in the park or by the sea, she walked alone. Just at a time when she most needed supportive companionship, no one was there.

Once the shock of Max's sudden death had passed and she had become more accustomed to her widowed state, Doreen's isolation became even more apparent. Playing bridge was one of her great pleasures, but the bridge club required you to attend with a partner – and Doreen didn't know anyone to ask. She didn't have the heart to join the horticultural society now that Max was not there to share the gardening with her. Eventually she could bear it no longer; she put the bungalow up for sale and returned to her former district and her circle of long-time friends.

Of course Max and Doreen's experience covers the worst possible scenario. There are many couples who retire and move away to spend a pleasant time together. But you do have to bear in mind that, happy as you may be with a partner, there is always the possibility that one or other of you may be left alone, and, if you have not had the time to get to know people in your new area, this could leave you lonely and isolated. Even moving to a district where a member of your family already lives may not provide the answer, as I know of at least two cases where, soon after this occurred, the adult child of the couple concerned was compelled for business reasons to move away.

This is not intended to be a 'doom and gloom' warning, but merely to ask you to think long and hard before uprooting yourself and moving to an entirely strange area. If you do decide to do so, then you should waste no time before getting to know local people, joining organisations or clubs etc. Decorating can come later.

Housebound people

If you are housebound for much of the time because of failing health or because you are differently abled, keeping in contact with people will naturally be more difficult. It is not impossible, however. Provided you are well enough to do so, you can keep in touch with others by correspondence – whether you prefer to communicate by written letter or spoken cassette. The pleasure this can bring is certainly well worth the cost of the postage. And I know several housebound people whose company is so delightful that they have no shortage of visitors to their homes.

Should you have a particular condition, there is usually a support group or organisation in existence designed specifically for you. Apart from keeping you up to date with any new developments or aids which may appear, there are often newsletters and additional means of keeping in touch with others who have the same condition.

Keeping contact

So, let's assume that you have decided it is important to maintain contact with other people even though you do not have a job. Let's also assume that you do not have a great deal of money to spare. What can you do?

Sometimes the answer lies in the extension of a hobby or interest you already have. Painting is great fun – so why not join a local group or class? This can be a formal class organised by your nearest adult education centre or you might just like to get together with a few friends with similar interests and form your own art group.

Gardening is an enjoyable and a healthy hobby and, if it interests you, you could join a local society. This might be a general one or a group devoted to a specific type of plant, such as fuchsias or alpines. Not only would you find people with the same interest as you, but swapping seeds and cuttings is a very inexpensive way of building up stocks of your favourite plants.

You may be a very active person who loves taking part in sport. However, clubs and leisure centres can prove quite expensive when cash is limited. Why not form an amateur team and set up friendly contests? Or you could take up walking which can be so much more pleasurable in the company of a friend – or even a group if you prefer it.

Music of all types can bring you great pleasure – whether you prefer to make it yourself or simply to listen to the work of others. Of course you can sit alone at your piano or beside your hi fi, but it is not difficult to arrange for a few others to be present with whom you can listen to and discuss your favourite kind of music – or who may even join you for a sing-song.

Even if you think you have no specific hobby or interest, for the cost of a few cups of coffee or tea you could spend time in the company of pleasant friends and talk about anything which interests you.

Whatever you decide to do, it will have the effect of reducing your sense of isolation and helping you to feel that you are part of a unit rather than someone who is 'different' or 'shut out'.

There are an enormous number of classes run by adult education centres and other organisations in almost every district. You will usually find that, if you are retired or unemployed, you will be able to enrol for these for minimal cost. So be adventurous and try something completely different. You may eventually decide that the particular subject is not for you, but you will certainly have met some new people and, perhaps just as importantly, have stretched your mind in new directions.

So many forms of voluntary work exist that, whatever your interests and your aptitudes, you are bound to be able to find an area in which you would enjoy working and where your help could prove invaluable.

You might choose to be in the 'front line' of helpers, giving your time to work with mentally or physically disabled people. Such work can be not only rewarding but fun also. One young man I know decided to offer his time and assistance to a home for children with physical and mental disabilities. Just before his first morning there, he confided that he was a little nervous, not knowing how he was going to cope with whatever he might find and how he would react to the various conditions which the children had. When I encountered him again, some two weeks later, he told me that he was having a wonderful time, and that the children were so open and responsive that he didn't feel like a 'helper' at all but more like a friend. In fact, so engrossed did he become in his efforts and so well did the children respond to him, that he gave up looking for the type of job he had previously been seeking in order to undertake training which would enable him to specialise in this type of work.

If physically caring for others in this way is not for you, perhaps you could assist in raising funds for whatever cause appeals to you. From hospices to the environment, animal welfare to Third World aid – all charities are desperate for increased funds and always looking for help in raising them. You can give as much or as little of your time as you choose – and in whatever way you choose. People are needed who are willing to stand in the High Street with collecting tins, to sell raffle tickets, to run stalls at fundraising fairs and sales. One friend of mine gives his time and effort by collecting for and selling goods at car boot sales, donating all the takings to his chosen charity.

There are also a number of charity shops in most towns. Indeed, the funds raised are heavily relied upon by such organisations as the Sue Ryder Foundation, Oxfam and Help the Aged. The manager of such shops is usually a paid member of staff – often with responsibility for several shops over a fairly wide area – but all other members of staff are volunteers. Some of these work regular hours, while others are available to step in should the need arise.

It may be that you do not wish, or are not able, to work in the shop itself, dealing with customers and handling money. Don't think that your help is not needed in other ways, however. Goods have to be sorted and priced. Minor repairs, such as sewing on buttons or fixing hems, may be needed. Some items may require ironing before being put on hangers. There is even a window-dressing job if the goods are to be displayed as attractively as possible so that prospective customers are encouraged to come into the shop. And they do come. There is now no social stigma involved in purchasing goods in charity shops – and rightly so as there are some good bargains to be had. Not only that, but by buying from these shops you help to conserve the resources of the world, while giving assistance to those helped by the particular charity concerned.

Perhaps you have always fancied yourself as a radio presenter. Opportunities exist here, too, which can be highly enjoyable while you are helping other people. The music and messages heard on hospital radio mean a great deal to those who are lying in the beds in the wards – particularly if they are finding it difficult to sleep. Volunteers are also needed to help with talking newspapers for visually impaired people. This usually involves keeping an eye on the local and national press, and cutting out anything which you think may be of interest to your listeners, and which is not of such major significance that it is bound to be covered by the regular bulletins on national radio. Then at regular intervals you record these items on to an audio-cassette and this is incorporated into the local talking newspaper. If you are interested in helping either with hospital radio or talking newspapers, you can obtain further information from your nearest hospital or the local Citizens' Advice Bureau.

BBC research has indicated that older people are under-represented in the media by one to three. This was brought to the fore by the Carnegie Inquiry's Report into the Third Age. The report also points out that broadcasting is really the one medium available in almost all retired households, and that it would therefore be the ideal means for presenting the ideas and experiences of older people.

Community Service Volunteers has a broadcasting section known as CSV Media, and a course was recently created by them to enable older and retired people to learn the skills of broadcasting which they can put to good use with local radio and television (with whom CSV Media often works in partnership).

You may choose to become more involved with your local community and its projects – from conservation to local politics. Not only will you find a fulfilling and interesting way of filling your time, but you will also be making your choice heard and hopefully improving conditions for others in your area. Here again the activities are as varied as the people wishing to take part in them. One person may wish to take part in their local Neighbourhood Watch scheme while another will seek to campaign for a prospective councillor. Or, for those who are energetic and strong enough, you might want to take part in environmental conservation schemes – which can involve anything from clearing rights of way to reclaiming or maintaining forest or meadow land (under the supervision of an environmental expert).

Here are some of the ways in which this sort of team work can improve your life while you are without a job.

● If you are in the process of looking for a job, the type of activity indicated in this chapter will certainly count towards the 'experience' so anxiously sought by any prospective employers. It can show that you are capable of using your time productively, have managerial skills, and have the needs and concerns of other people at heart. And someone who is willing to make such efforts for the local community will probably be as willing to make efforts for the employing company.

• For those who have been out of the world of work for some time, taking part in the ventures described will help to rebuild your confidence. You will come to accept the fact that your efforts are as valuable as those of anyone else and that you have a great deal to offer. This, in turn, will be obvious when you write a letter of application or attend an interview. There is an old saying that 'If you don't value yourself, how can you expect anyone else to do so?'

• If you have retired, you will have the opportunity to feel – and be – truly useful again. You have a lifetime of skills and experience which can prove invaluable in many different areas, and here is your chance to demonstrate them. You may prefer the safety of sticking to what you already know or you may find it exciting and stimulating to respond to the challenge of trying something completely new.

• Many people these days live alone – members of their family often being several hours' journey away. Team work of the type described will provide you with colleagues, friends and acquaintances; this will enable you to feel that you 'belong' again, and to increase and improve your social life too.

• You will discover how much can be done with only a very small (or sometimes no) financial outlay. The pleasure and satisfaction derived in no way bears a relation to the money expended – and, if you are without a job, this is often a highly significant consideration.

—— 139 ——

Finding that you are forced to survive without a job, you are faced with a choice. There are two paths you can take: you can decide to withdraw from the world and wait for circumstances to overtake you; or you can get up, get out there and get going!

If you choose the former, what is likely to happen? You will sit at home, feeling more despondent, more unwanted and more depressed. Even if you put a great deal of effort into writing letters and filling in application forms, we all know that you will receive replies to only a few of these. Lack of response – or negative replies – are far easier to cope with when you have others with whom you can share the information. When you face them alone the rejection feels as though it is aimed at you personally rather than being a sign of the current national situation.

The more depressed and disgruntled you grow, the harder you will find it to relate and respond to others should the situation arise. You will be classed as 'poor company' and will be treated as such or even left completely alone. Human nature being as it is, this will then increase your belief in your own lack of self-worth and you will have stepped on to a negative treadmill from which it is very difficult to escape.

That is one choice. Of course, should you elect to continue living your life as fully as possible, albeit without the benefit of a job, what is the outcome likely to be? You will be able to enjoy the company of other people which will help to reduce any sense of isolation you may have been experiencing. However much you may have been feeling that you were 'unwanted' or 'rejected', you will now realise that you are extremely useful, and that your time and effort are appreciated.

Even if you do not join in any activity as a means of finding a job, networking is always positive and you never know when someone you encounter can lead to a work-related contact. And we have already acknowledged that all experience is valid so that, for those seeking employment, you have something to put on your CV which might well give you that extra advantage when needed.

Perhaps the most important thing of all is that your self-esteem will improve and your confidence increase. You will like yourself and realise that you are a person with a great deal to offer. This will enable you to carry with you an aura of positivity which will be obvious to anyone with whom you come into contact. They, in turn, will react towards you in a positive way, increasing your confidence still further and, instead of that negative treadmill, you will find yourself on a delightful upward spiral.

If you have been feeling miserable because you are without a job, make this the moment you begin to do something to change those feelings. Whether you hope to be employed in the future, wish to set up in self-employment or know that that particular part of your life has come to an end, there is a whole world of people and experiences out there just waiting for you to join it. Life may be different – but it can be pleasurable and fulfilling if you let it. Let this be the moment of change which will enable you to live every moment of that life.

— 10 —

Where to look

Much information is to be found at your local reference library or Citizens' Advice Bureau, but here are some specific names and addresses you might find useful. As many of these organis-ations work on a small budget and all of them have an enormous postage bill, where possible enclose a self-addressed stamped envelope when writing to them.

—— *Personal development* ——

For details of courses in such subjects as assertiveness and confi-dence, contact your local reference library or the Enterprise Unit (usually attached to your local adult education centre).

The British Association for Counselling
37a Sheep Street
Rugby, Warwickshire CV21 3BX
(0788 578328)

BOOKS AND PUBLICATIONS

Assert Yourself by Gael Lindenfield (Thorsons).
Learned Optimism by Dr Martin Seligman (Knopf).
Living with Change by Ursula Markham (Element Books).
Managing Stress by Ursula Markham (Element Books).
Strategies of Optimism by Vera Peiffer (Element Books).

CASSETTES

'Relax and Gain Confidence' is available from:
Thorsons Cassette Dept
78–85 Fulham Palace Road
London W6 8JB

An extensive range of self-help and personal development cassettes is available from:
The Hypnothink Foundation
PO Box 154
Cheltenham, Gloucestershire
GL53 9EG
(s.a.e. for full list)

— *Redundancy and employment* —

Information on redundancy and employment law is available from your local Employment Department Service.

If you feel your dismissal was unfair and you wish to contest it, contact the local branch of ACAS (Advisory, Conciliation and Arbitration Service). Their number is in your local telephone directory.

The Training and Enterprise Council (TEC) for your area will be able to advise you on the Enterprise Allowance Scheme, career development loans and grants, as well as opportunities for retraining.

REACH (Retired Executives Action Clearing House) is a charity which tries to match retired executives with voluntary organisations. Their address is:
89 Southwark Street
London SE1 0HD
(071–928 0452)

BOOKS AND PUBLICATIONS

Running Your Own Business by Richard Edwards (Longman).

———— *Retirement and age* ————

The Association of Retired Persons
Parnell House
Wilton Road
London SW1V 1LW
(071–895 8880)

Pre-Retirement Association
19 Undine Street
London SW17 8PP
(081–767 3225)

Age Concern
65 Pitcairn Road
Mitcham, Surrey
CR4 3LI
(081–640 5431)

Centre for Policy on Ageing
25/31 Ironmonger Row
London EC1V 3QP
(071–253 1787)

University of the Third Age
1 Stockwell Green
London SW9 9JF
(071–737 2541)

BOOKS AND PUBLICATIONS

Approaching Retirement (Consumers' Association).
Ourselves, Growing Older by Paula Brown Doress and Diana
Laskin, edited by Jean Shapiro (Fontana).
The Good Retirement Guide by Rosemary Brown
(Bloomsbury).

—— *Returning to Education* ——

For a handbook, advice and application form on becoming a
mature student, contact:
UCAS (Universities and Colleges Admissions Service)
PO Box 28
Cheltenham, Gloucestershire
GL50 3SA

The Open University
PO Box 71
Milton Keynes MK7 6AG
(0908 274066)

The Council for the Accreditation of Correspondence Colleges
27 Marylebone Road
London NW1 5JS

BOOKS AND PUBLICATIONS

Second Chances published by COIC (Careers and Occupational Information Centre). Contact 0742 753275 or your local reference library.

The Kogan Page Mature Student's Handbook by Margaret Korving (Kogan Page).

Women returners

Women Returners' Network
Chelmsford Adult Education Centre
Patching Hall Lane
Chelmsford, Essex CM1 4DB
(0245 358631)

The Pepperell Unit at The Industrial Society
48 Bryanston Square
London W1H 7LN
(071–262 2401)

BOOKS AND PUBLICATIONS

The Women Returners' Network Directory (Longman).
Women Under Pressure by Ursula Markham (Element Books).

General

For further information about Probus Clubs in your area, contact the local Rotary Club or your reference library.

CSV Media (Broadcasting skills)
237 Pentonville Road
London N1 9NJ
(071–278 6601)

The Market Dept
National Federation of Women's Institutes (selling produce)
104 New King's Road
London SW6 4LY
071–371 9300

National Council for Voluntary Organisations
26 Bedford Square
London WC1B 3HU
(071–636 4066)

BOOKS AND PUBLICATIONS

Making Money from your Garden by Barty Phillips (Piatkus Books).

Index

THE PERFECT CV
How to get the job you really want
Tom Jackson

Finding a job is easier than you think.

The Perfect CV is the essential book for all jobhunters at every stage of their career. It will show you how to:

- define your most marketable skills
- identify what you really enjoy doing
- demonstrate proven abilities
- set out your abilities and accomplishments in a way that impresses future employers

The Perfect CV includes over 50 examples of job-winning CVs and hundreds of job ideas. It is the definitive guide to job-hunting.

PERFECT JOB SEARCH STRATEGIES
Over 100 proven strategies for getting the job you want in today's challenging market
Tom Jackson

This unique book is your guide to solving every major career-finding dilemma. It is a book of proven and practical solutions and strategies that will keep you on target at every stage of your job search.

Perfect Job Search Strategies has been specially designed to give you on-the-spot answers to more than 100 situations, challenges and turning points in your search for the job you want. Use it as an interactive guide to intelligent action at each step on the way. If you have ever felt that your career search was in a rut, this is the book for you!

MARKETING YOURSELF
How to sell yourself and get the jobs you've always wanted
Dorothy Leeds

Marketing Yourself is packed with advice on how to present yourself and your abilities to future employers in the most effective way. It shows you how to:

- Plan your career – whether you're going for your first job or your tenth
- Turn your major sales assets into selling points
- Recognise and maximise your 10 most marketable skills – the ones which every employer is looking for
- Write the perfect CV and tailor it to each job application
- Control your job interviews from beginning to end
- Negotiate for what you want – and get it

Marketing Yourself will help you to be among the top contenders for every job you apply for.

Dorothy Leeds is the president of a management consultancy firm and she develops and conducts management and sales seminars.